Eating Disorders

Eating Disorders

JEFF HILL

LUCENT BOOKS

A part of Gale, Cengage Learning

GALE
CENGAGE Learning·

Detroit • New York • San Francisco • New Haven, Conn • Waterville, Maine • London

LIBRARY OF CONGRESS CATALOGING-IN-PUBLICATION DATA

Hill, Jeff, 1962-
  Eating disorders / by Jeff Hill.
    p. cm. -- (Nutrition and health)
  Includes bibliographical references and index.
  ISBN 978-1-4205-0719-5 (hardcover)
  1. Eating disorders. 2. Eating disorders--Risk factors. 3. Eating disorders--Treatment. I. Title.
  RC552.E18H533 2013
  616.85'26--dc23

                                                        2012020004

Lucent Books
27500 Drake Rd.
Farmington Hills, MI 48331

ISBN-13: 978-1-4205-0719-5
ISBN-10: 1-4205-0719-2

Printed in the United States of America
1 2 3 4 5 6 7 16 15 14 13 12

TABLE OF CONTENTS

Many people today are often amazed by the amount of nutrition and health information, often contradictory, that can be found in the media. Television, newspapers, and magazines bombard readers with the latest news and recommendations. Television news programs report on recent scientific studies. The healthy living sections of newspapers and magazines offer information and advice. In addition, electronic media such as websites, blogs, and forums post daily nutrition and health news and recommendations.

This constant stream of information can be confusing. The science behind nutrition and health is constantly evolving. Current research often leads to new ideas and insights. Many times, the latest nutrition studies and health recommendations contradict previous studies or traditional health advice. When the media reports these changes without giving context or explanations, consumers become confused. In a survey by the National Health Council, for example, 68 percent of participants agreed that "when reporting medical and health news, the media often contradict themselves, so I don't know what to believe." In addition, the Food Marketing Institute reported that eight out of ten consumers thought it was likely that nutrition and health experts would have a completely different idea about what foods are healthy within five years. With so much contradictory information, people have difficulty deciding how to apply nutrition and health recommendations to their lives. Students find it difficult to find relevant, yet clear and credible information for reports.

Changing recommendations for antioxidant supplements are an example of how confusion can arise. In the 1990s antioxidants such as vitamins C and E and beta-carotene came to the public's attention. Scientists found that people who ate more antioxidant-rich foods had a lower risk of heart disease, cancer, vision loss, and other chronic conditions than those who ate lower amounts. Without waiting for more scientific study, the media and supplement companies quickly spread the word that antioxidants could help fight and prevent disease. They recommended that people take antioxidant supplements and eat fortified foods. When further scientific studies were completed, however, most did not support the initial recommendations. While naturally occurring antioxidants in fruits and vegetables may help prevent a variety of chronic diseases, little scientific evidence proved antioxidant supplements had the same effect. In fact, a study published in the November 2008 *Journal of the American Medical Association* found that supplemental vitamins A and C gave no more heart protection than a placebo. The study's results contradicted the widely publicized recommendation, leading to consumer confusion. This example highlights the importance of context for evaluating nutrition and health news. Understanding a topic's scientific background, interpreting a study's findings, and evaluating news sources are critical skills that help reduce confusion.

Lucent's Nutrition and Health series is designed to help young people sift through the mountain of confusing facts, opinions, and recommendations. Each book contains the most recent up-to-date information, synthesized and written so that students can understand and think critically about nutrition and health issues. Each volume of the series provides a balanced overview of today's hot-button nutrition and health issues while presenting the latest scientific findings and a discussion of issues surrounding the topic. The series provides young people with tools for evaluating conflicting and ever-changing ideas about nutrition and health. Clear narrative peppered with personal anecdotes, fully documented primary and secondary source quotes, informative sidebars, fact boxes, and statistics are all used to help readers understand these topics and how they affect their bodies and their lives. Each volume includes information about changes in trends over time, political controversies, and international perspectives. Full-color photographs and charts enhance all volumes in the series. The Nutrition and Health series is a valuable resource for young people to understand current topics and make informed choices for themselves.

Mysterious and Misunderstood Illnesses

When anorexia nervosa was first identified as a distinct condition in the 1870s, descriptions of people who willingly starved themselves—sometimes to the point of death—seemed strange and shocking. People had a very difficult time understanding a condition that defied one of the most basic human needs and desires: the consumption of food.

Today, eating disorders are no longer a novel subject. They are often discussed in the media and widely studied by doctors. The increased attention paid to eating disorders in the past half century has resulted in the identification of new conditions, including bulimia nervosa and binge-eating disorder. Despite all of these developments, though, eating disorders are still in many ways misunderstood.

The general public often views eating disorders in simple terms that distort the reality of what an affected individual experiences. Many people assume the disorders are merely diets that have gotten out of control, and that the behavior can be easily overcome by convincing or forcing the patient to eat. Other misconceptions are focused on common characteristics of individuals with eating disorders. Because they are frequently young and are obsessed with their weight, they are sometimes dismissed as vain and self-centered adolescents. Such opinions seem to suggest that an eating disorder is just a difficult phase that will end once the individual realizes that he or she needs to grow up. Moreover, media accounts often present the treatment process as a simple and relatively brief experience in which a patient completes a program and returns to normal life completely cured.

The truth is that anorexia, bulimia, and other related behaviors are serious psychological disorders. Although they may be focused on the subject of food, these conditions are usually caused by some deeper source of stress in the individual's life. As a result, overcoming these ailments is not a simple matter of giving up a diet or adopting a more mature outlook. While effective treatments are available, there are no miracle cures. Recovery is typically a slow and difficult process, with many setbacks along the way.

A young girl with bulimia purges. Bulimia, anorexia, and other eating disorders are considered serious psychological disorders.

As tough as it can be to recover from an eating disorder, the alternative is grim. An eating disorder is a life-threatening condition. If left untreated, it can have severe and long-lasting effects on a person's health. Anorexia nervosa, in particular, is one of the most deadly of all psychological illnesses. With determination, commitment, and effective treatment, however, many people successfully overcome eating disorders—and their inspiring stories can provide a source of hope and strength for others engaged in similar struggles.

CHAPTER 1

Eating Disorders and the People They Affect

The scale is waiting when you come home from school. The scale is always waiting. You tentatively step on, and red neon numbers blink back at you. Down three pounds [1.3kg]. Hands shaking, eyes red, you're breathing rapidly and your heart is on overdrive, thumping against the confines of your rib cage.

You wake up in the night, almost every night, terrified that you've gained weight. At three o'clock on a frigid winter morning, you leave the nest of your blanketed bed and slide out of flannel pajamas. Shivering, you pull the scale out from its hiding place under your bed and step on. You haven't gained ten pounds [4.5kg] in your sleep. You go back to bed.[1]

The above quotation, from Nicole Johns's memoir *Purge,* offers a chilling description of one young woman's experience living with an eating disorder. The term "eating disorder" can refer to a number of different behaviors and mental health issues, but they all hinge on a central problem: an extreme preoccupation with weight, body image, and eating. "Extreme" is the key word, because nearly everyone is interested in their physical appearance to some degree, and these concerns often focus on weight and fitness. Many people follow restricted-calorie diets in hopes of becoming slimmer, for instance, and many people participate in activities such as running and bicycling with the goal of losing weight. Most individuals who attempt to control their weight do so without causing serious harm to their health, though they may or may not succeed in their quest to shed pounds.

For others, however, the idea of losing weight can become entangled with other factors and lead to the development of an eating disorder. People with eating disorders fixate on what they eat, how much they weigh, and the appearance of their bodies until these subjects come to dominate their lives. Moreover, their attempts to control these factors severely impact their health and can even threaten their lives.

Numerous factors can affect a person's eating behavior. In the opinion of most experts, however, eating disorders are not

People with eating disorders often obsessively check their weight.

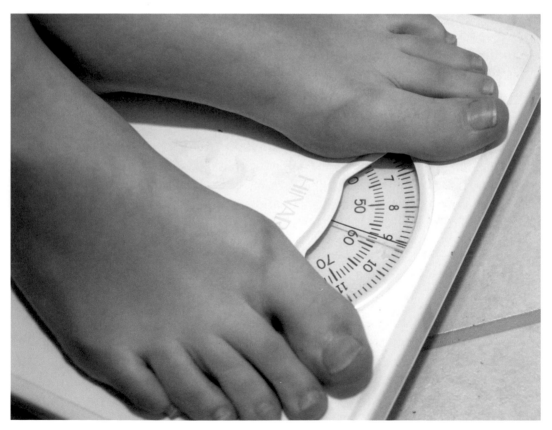

simply the outcome of a wish to become thinner. Instead, they are a response to difficult circumstances in a person's life, and the problems that trigger the disorder may be only partially related to the issues of food and fitness. "Eating disorders run much deeper than simply a child's desire to lose weight," note Pamela Carlton and Deborah Ashin in *Take Charge of Your Child's Eating Disorder*. "Most eating disorders reflect a child's coping mechanisms—albeit maladaptive [unhealthy] ones—to deal with external stresses."[2]

Eating Disorders: A Brief Overview

Doctors have defined two primary types of eating disorders, anorexia nervosa and bulimia nervosa. Anorexia nervosa can be described as a "relentless pursuit of excessive thinness,"[3] according to psychologist Hilde Bruch, a pioneer in the study of eating disorders. People affected by this disorder severely limit their intake of food to the point where they become extremely underweight. Their condition is sometimes made worse by excessive exercise and purging (vomiting or misusing laxatives, diuretics, and enemas in an effort to rid the body of food that has been consumed). In addition, people with anorexia nervosa have such distorted perceptions of their weight and body shape that they are unable to accurately assess their condition.

The second major type of eating disorder, bulimia nervosa, is marked by uncontrolled eating binges that are accompanied by purging, excessive exercise, or fasting in an attempt to prevent weight gain. Because bulimia involves the ingestion of calories as well as harmful means of eliminating them, people affected by the disorder may remain at or near their normal body weight, even while experiencing other serious health problems as a result of their behavior.

Doctors employ a list of criteria to decide whether an individual should be diagnosed with anorexia or bulimia.

Anorexia is described as a "relentless pursuit of excessive thinness" by psychologist Hilde Bruch.

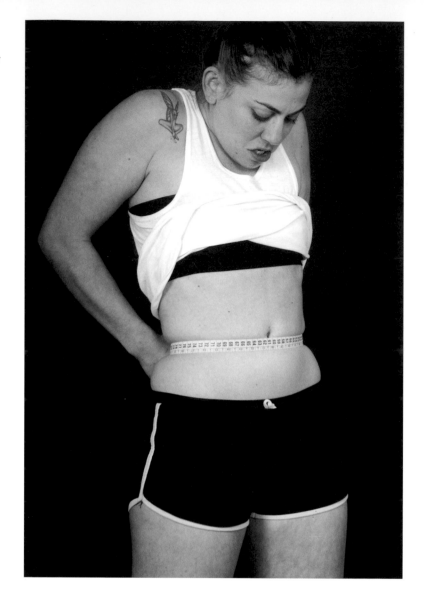

Health care providers have also recognized that many people demonstrate some elements of disordered eating behavior even though they do not meet all of the criteria required for a diagnosis of anorexia or bulimia. They created a third classification, eating disorder not otherwise specified (EDNOS), to help identify and treat such cases.

Although most eating disorders revolve around an individual's efforts to lose weight, there is one notable exception. Binge-eating disorder (BED), which is classified as part of the EDNOS category, occurs when a person engages in uncontrolled eating binges but does not attempt to purge, exercise, or fast to prevent weight gain, as is the case with bulimia. As a result, people affected by BED frequently become overweight. The subject of obesity—an excessive amount of body fat—is sometimes considered in conjunction with eating disorders. There are many factors that contribute to being overweight, however—not all of which are related to a psychological eating disorder.

Medically speaking, all eating disorders are considered to be psychological rather than physiological disorders. This distinction means that eating disorders are caused by an individual's mental processes, rather than by some kind of physical problem with the body. On the other hand, some experts believe that physical factors may contribute to eating disorders. For example, some studies have suggested that people's genetic make-up or body chemistry may make them more likely to develop an eating disorder. Such theories have not yet been conclusively proven, however, and research into the subject is ongoing.

Modern Disorders with Ancient Roots

Although eating disorders have only become the subject of extensive research in recent decades, they have been documented over many centuries. There are accounts of people purposefully denying themselves food as early as A.D. 400. In some cases, individuals who avoided eating were thought to be possessed by demons. In other cases, they were seen as miraculous figures inspired by great religious devotion. Saint Catherine of Siena, a Catholic saint who lived in Italy in the 1300s, was known to undertake extended fasts throughout her life. She also reportedly engaged in behavior common to modern people with eating disorders, such as secretly throwing her food under the dining table rather than eating it.

The English physician Richard Morton provided the first clinical description of what would later become known as anorexia nervosa in the late 1600s. Though he termed the condition "nervous consumption,"[4] he noted most of the classic symptoms of the disorder, including avoidance of food, weight loss, hyperactivity, and patients' apparent disregard for their own health. The term anorexia nervosa—which literally means nervous loss of appetite—came into being in the 1870s through the work of two physicians, Sir William Gull in England and Charles Lasègue in France. In the decades that followed, doctors tended to attribute anorexia to medical factors, such as problems with the pituitary gland. By the mid-1900s, however, the disorder was being treated primarily as a form of mental illness.

Many experts believe that eating disorders have become much more common since the 1950s, though others dispute this point. Whether or not there has been a true increase in the number of people affected by eating disorders, there has certainly been an increase in professional analysis of the ailments. The additional scientific research and medical attention given to eating disorders resulted in the identification of bulimia nervosa as a separate disorder in 1979. Media

The Miraculous Maids

In the late 1800s newspapers around the world published sensational tales of women who claimed to live for long periods without eating. Known as "fasting girls" and "miraculous maids," these individuals became the source of heated debate. Some people claimed that they proved the existence of some type of higher spiritual power, while others insisted that they instead suffered from psychological ailments—what was then called hysteria.

Mollie Fancher of Brooklyn, New York, was one of the best known of these figures. She was said to have eaten only a few spoonfuls of milk and wine, a banana, and a cracker over the course of twelve years. In her book *The Fasting Girl,* historian Michelle Stacey argues that Fancher was suffering from anorexia nervosa, though she most certainly ate more than was claimed.

Other miraculous maids may have been affected by eating disorders as well, though several were revealed to be outright frauds. One of the most tragic figures was Sarah Jacob of Wales. At the age of twelve or fourteen (sources differ as to her age), she claimed to have lived for sixteen months without eating, and her account stirred a widespread debate about whether or not she was being truthful. In December 1869 her parents agreed to let a team of nurses launch a round-the-clock watch of the girl to verify whether or not she consumed food. During that period, at least, she ate nothing. She starved to death in eight days.

English physician Robert Morton provided the first clinical description of anorexia nervosa in the late 1600s.

coverage of eating disorders has also grown tremendously over the years. Since the death of singer Karen Carpenter from anorexia in 1983, popular magazines have been full of stories about celebrities who have struggled with eating disorders, including reality-TV personality Nicole Richie, actress Mary-Kate Olsen, model Kate Moss, and England's Princess Diana.

Who Develops Eating Disorders?

Medical researchers have analyzed data concerning the members of the population who have developed eating disorders. These studies have established a few widely accepted facts, but they have also inspired a great deal of debate and uncertainty. The varying views stem from the unique characteristics of the disorders. Eating disorders are relatively rare

A general consensus has been reached on some aspects of eating disorders, including the factors of gender, age, socioeconomic status, education, culture, and ethnicity.

in the general population, and that rarity makes them difficult to measure with great accuracy. In addition, individuals affected by eating disorders often try to hide their condition, so the number of reported cases tends to be lower than the actual number of people who have disorders. As a result, scientific studies that measure eating disorders often end up with somewhat different findings. Experts have reached a general consensus about some aspects of eating disorders, though, including the impact of gender, age, socioeconomic status, education, culture, and ethnicity on a person's likelihood of developing a disorder.

Eating Disorders and Young Women

Since the earliest medical studies of eating disorders were conducted in the late 1800s, doctors have been aware of one of the most startling features of the disorders: Young women are affected to a much greater degree than any other segment of the population. That fact has been confirmed by research studies conducted in recent decades. For nearly all forms of eating disorders, most experts believe that about 90 percent of those affected are female. "Young females are by far the most vulnerable group," notes Carlos M. Grilo in *Eating and Weight Disorders*. "This gender discrepancy is one of the most extreme of any medical or psychiatric problem."[5]

The peak years for the development of anorexia in girls are mid- to late-adolescence, roughly ages 14 through 18. Bulimia most commonly affects a slightly older age group, with the peak incidence taking place between ages 15 and 19.

Eating Disorders Among Other Demographic Groups

Medical researchers have generally found that about one out of every ten people with an eating disorder is male. Some recent studies have suggested that the disorders are becoming more common among boys and men, however, and certain authorities argue that males account for a higher percentage of eating disorders than traditionally recognized. This theory is based on research conducted in specific communities that has found that males make up between 15 and 30 percent of people with eating disorders. In addition, some specialists argue that many men and boys with eating disorders go uncounted, both because doctors are less likely to diagnose them with an eating disorder and because males are less likely to seek help in the first place. Research has indicated that gay men may be at a higher risk for developing an eating disorder, as are men employed in jobs where thinness is valued, including models, jockeys, and dancers.

Among both genders, the majority of people with eating disorders are adolescents and young adults. Although older individuals do experience eating disorders, there is a lack of precise data on how many people are affected in middle adulthood and beyond. Some experts believe that the problem is more widespread than statistics indicate, and that the numbers are growing. Researchers assert that in many cases, older people affected by an eating disorder initially formed an unhealthy relationship with food in their youth.

Socioeconomic Status and Education

In the mid-20th century, researchers thought that eating disorders primarily affected people from the middle and upper classes. Hilde Bruch's description of anorexia as a disease experienced by "young and healthy girls who have been raised in privileged, even luxurious circumstances"[6] is typical of this view. The theory that well-to-do families are more susceptible to eating disorders has come under criticism in recent years, however.

Critics of this theory assert that medical professionals have often misdiagnosed cases of eating disorders among individuals of lower socioeconomic status (SES), believing their less-affluent patients to be suffering from poor nutrition or some other health problem rather than an eating disorder. In addition, wealthy individuals are more likely to be in a position to seek and afford medical treatment for their disorders, so they may be better represented in the treatment programs on which many studies are based.

Other researchers continue to see trends related to social class and income levels among people affected by eating disorders. Some studies suggest that anorexia is more common among those of higher SES, while bulimia is more evenly distributed among all groups. In addition, certain studies have found that people of higher educational achievement are at a greater risk for eating disorders. This theory stems from research that has shown a higher rate of eating disorders among university populations compared with the general public. A 2002 study of college students, for instance, found that 4.5 percent of the women and 1.4 percent of the men reported previous treatment for an eating disorder.

Culture and Ethnicity

Culture also plays a role in determining the likelihood of people being affected by eating disorders. Eating disorders

The Male Aversion to Seeking Help for a Disorder

Statistics may underestimate the number of men with eating disorders because men tend to avoid seeking psychological help out of embarrassment or fear of appearing weak. Nevertheless, men and women alike are unlikely to recover without professional assistance. "Most individuals with eating disorders require therapy. Many men feel shy or awkward about seeking outside help, and therefore do not get the professional treatment they need," explain the authors of *Making Weight: Men's Conflicts with Food, Weight, Shape, and Appearance.* "But these disorders have numerous medical and emotional side effects, and only experienced professionals have the tools to help. If you have an eating disorder, unless you are the kind of guy who builds his own house, performs dental procedures on himself, *and* is his own lawyer, you need to get professional guidance!"

Arnold Andersen, Leigh Cohn, and Thomas Holbrook. *Making Weight: Men's Conflicts with Food, Weight, Shape, and Appearance.* Carlsbad, CA: Gürze, 2000, p. 208.

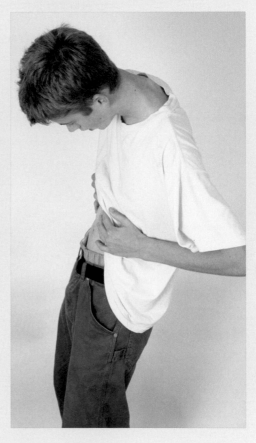

Many males with eating disorders are reluctant to seek outside help.

are far more common in Western, economically developed countries than elsewhere in the world. The United States, Canada, Australia, and nations in Europe have historically held the largest concentrations of cases. Eating disorders are therefore viewed as "culture-bound syndromes," because the values and way of life in certain countries seem to contribute to their development. Many different elements of culture may figure in this phenomenon, but one of the most important is the high value that Western nations place on thinness and physical fitness as the ideal of beauty.

Eating disorders have been documented in other nations, however, and some studies indicate that the number of people affected by eating disorders is climbing throughout the world. Japan, for example, has experienced increasing problems with eating-related disorders. Japanese society has adopted many aspects of Western culture, which may help

Statistical evidence suggests that Caucasians are more likely to develop eating disorders than are other ethnic and racial groups.

explain why its residents have a high rate of eating disorders. Similar trends have been noted in areas of China, India, and Malaysia that have seen a great deal of Western-oriented development.

The issue of how race and ethnicity affect the likelihood of developing eating disorders has been widely examined as well. Some statistical evidence indicates that Caucasians are more likely to develop eating disorders than other groups, while African Americans and Hispanics have a particularly low incidence of eating disorders. It is not known whether genetic factors explain these differences, or whether some ethnic groups simply tend to place less emphasis on thinness than others. Some analysts argue that such findings may be misleading because cases of eating disorders among minorities are more likely to be misdiagnosed or go untreated.

Prevalence and Trends

Eating disorders are not widespread among the general population, but some types are more common than others.

Anorexia nervosa is the rarest of the disorders. The prevalence (the proportion of people in the general population who are affected) of anorexia has been estimated at around 0.1 percent. In other words, statistics indicate that only one person out of every one thousand has anorexia. This figure is not very precise, however, because people with anorexia typically attempt to hide their condition and because it is difficult to accurately measure such a rare disorder in the general population.

Attempts to gauge the number of cases among young females—the group most often affected by anorexia—are thought to be more accurate, though the numbers still vary among sources. One of the most commonly cited statistics indicates that one out of every two hundred females ages fifteen through nineteen is anorexic, which equals 0.5 percent, though other studies have settled on a lower figure of 0.3 percent.

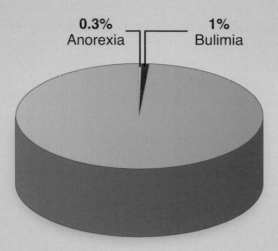
Researchers also debate whether anorexia has become more common in the past half century. Several prominent studies found that the number of new cases increased between the mid-1900s and the 1980s, but leveled off in the decades since. On the other hand, some eating-disorder experts argue that there were problems with the research studies that came to these conclusions. These critics point out that the rise in diagnosed cases of anorexia could be caused by the increased attention that has been focused on the disorder in recent decades.

Bulimia nervosa is generally believed to be about twice as common as anorexia. Most sources estimate that between 1 and 2 percent of young females are affected by the disorder. Although other research has yielded higher numbers, some of those studies have defined bulimia nervosa more loosely. Some studies, for example, have counted individuals who have had any type of bulimic episode, rather than those who would meet all of the requirements for a professional diagnosis of bulimia.

Many health authorities believe that there was a sharp increase in the number of people affected by bulimia beginning in the 1970s, with a particularly large spike occurring after bulimia was recognized as a separate psychological disorder in the late 1970s. Following that period of sudden increase, the number of bulimia cases has stabilized.

The disorders that fall under the category of eating disorder not otherwise specified have received less study than anorexia and bulimia. As a result, there are fewer precise statistics available about the prevalence of EDNOS in the general population. More people are diagnosed with

HEALTH FACT

Studies have found that about 20 percent of all women have engaged in episodes of uncontrolled binge eating.

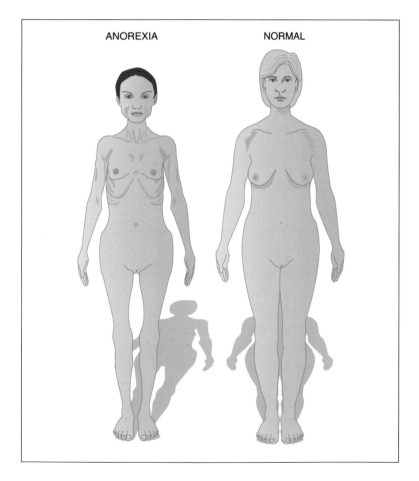

Artwork shows a severely underweight woman with anorexia nervosa and a woman of healthy weight. Statistics indicate one out of every two hundred females aged fifteen to nineteen are anorexic.

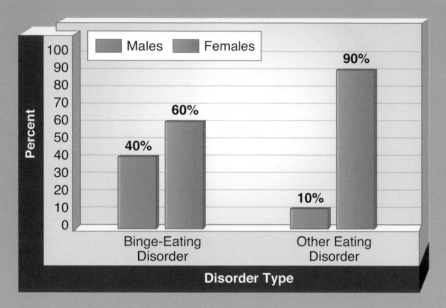

Ratio of Male Patients Among Disorder Types

Percent (y-axis: 0, 10, 20, 30, 40, 50, 60, 70, 80, 90, 100)

Legend: Males, Females

Binge-Eating Disorder: 40% (Males), 60% (Females)
Other Eating Disorder: 10% (Males), 90% (Females)

Disorder Type

Taken from: Terence M. Dovey. *Eating Behaviour.* Maidenhead, UK: Open University Press, 2010, p.140; Carlos M. Grilo. *Eating and Weight Disorders.* Hove, UK: Psychology, 2006, p. 36.

EDNOS than with the other two disorders, however. Two studies from the 2000s found that EDNOS patients made up 60 to 70 percent of those being treated for eating disorders.

Some of the research conducted on binge-eating disorder indicates that it is different from other eating disorders in certain respects. It is the most common of the specifically defined disorders, with one study estimating that it affects about 3 percent of the general population. It is also more evenly distributed between men and women, with a ratio of 1.5 females to 1 male. Finally, it seems to be much more common in adults than it is in children and adolescents. Information on binge-eating disorder is rather limited, however, since it has only recently been identified as a distinct eating disorder.

Researchers have observed a number of facts and statistical trends about who is most likely to be affected by eating disorders. It is important to note, however, that eating disorders can be found among all types of people. No age group, gender, social class, or ethnic group can be considered immune. Individuals from all walks of life and from many parts of the world grapple with these difficult ailments—and the related threats to their health—on a daily basis.

CHAPTER 2

Types, Characteristics, and Dangers of Eating Disorders

In her book *Lying in Weight,* Trisha Gura describes the feelings of anxiety, insecurity, and loneliness that often plague people affected by eating disorders. "I have a voice in my head that whispers like a ghost. It seduces. It tells me that no one will love me if I am fat," she writes. "It promises that if I follow its rules, skipping meals, swimming extra laps, not eating this or that, avoiding meat and chicken and fish and dairy products, I will be safe. But most of the time I do not feel safe—just closed up and isolated."[7]

Because an individual's underlying emotions play such a significant role, eating disorders are medically classified as psychological or mental health disorders. As a result, the standard definitions associated with the main types of eating disorders—anorexia nervosa, bulimia nervosa, and eating disorder not otherwise specified (EDNOS)—are taken from the *Diagnostic and Statistical Manual of Mental Disorders (DSM),* published by the American Psychological Association. This publication lists all of the psychological disorders that are officially recognized by the American medical community and defines them with specific criteria. The manual's guidelines are widely used by health care providers, and they provide a useful means for gaining a basic understanding of the illnesses.

Anorexia Nervosa

According to the 2000 edition of the *DSM* (the most current edition as of this printing), there are four major characteristics that must be met for a doctor to make a diagnosis of anorexia nervosa:

1. Body weight 15 percent or more below normal.
To analyze a patient's weight, doctors determine his or her body mass index (BMI). BMI is a number that is calculated using a person's weight and height. BMI accounts for the fact that a taller person has a larger body frame than a shorter person, and thus should be expected to weigh more. When assessing whether a patient is underweight, medical professionals also consider their gender, because males and females develop differently. Age is also taken into consideration, because weight can vary greatly depending on a person's stage of physical development. For children and teenagers, a BMI figure that is less than 85 percent of what is considered normal for their height, gender, and age is a possible warning sign of anorexia. Although being underweight is one element of the diagnosis, the patient must also meet the other criteria listed below.

2. Intense fear of gaining weight.
Individuals affected by anorexia experience malnutrition because they are obsessed with controlling their weight. Unlike BMI, which can be measured objectively, the degree to which a person worries about becoming heavier cannot be determined precisely. Instead, a doctor attempts to understand the individual's feelings by conducting a psychological assessment that includes an in-depth interview.

3. Disturbed perception of body weight and shape.
One of the most striking aspects of anorexia is the distorted manner in which affected individuals perceive their own physical condition. Some people are simply unable to accurately assess their weight and shape, which causes them to believe that they are overweight when they are not. This perception can persist regardless of how thin they become. As a result, people with anorexia often insist that they need to lose weight even as they experience the

effects of starvation. "Even as I watched the numbers drop on the scale and dropped clothing sizes, I couldn't see the difference in the mirror,"[8] notes Carrie Arnold, who began struggling with the disorder in her teens.

Other people affected by anorexia may be able to accurately judge their weight loss, but they view their emaciated condition as a positive development. They typically deny the severe medical problems that can be caused by starvation, and they may lie about how they perceive their weight in hopes of avoiding treatment. This view is reflected by a

HEALTH FACT

According to the U.S. Centers for Disease Control and Prevention (CDC), the following weight ranges are considered healthy for fifteen-year-olds of the heights specified. The CDC cautions individuals whose weight falls below this range to see a health care provider to be evaluated for a possible eating disorder.

Fifteen-year-old girl:

Height	Healthy Weight Range
5 feet, 0 inches	84–122 pounds
5 feet, 3 inches	92–135 pounds
5 feet, 6 inches	101–148 pounds

Fifteen-year-old boy:

Height	Healthy Weight Range
5 feet, 0 inches	85–119 pounds
5 feet, 3 inches	94–132 pounds
5 feet, 6 inches	103–145 pounds

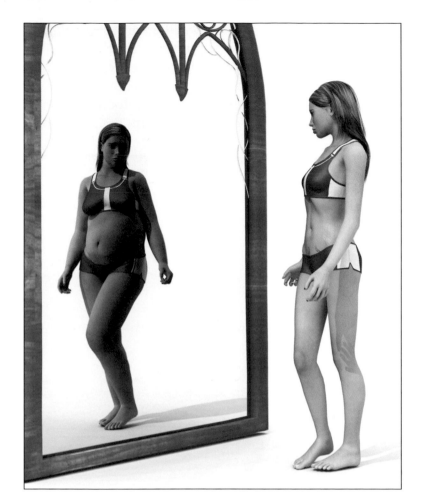

Anorexia nervosa can cause individuals to perceive their bodies in a distorted manner.

woman who admits that she knew she was dangerously thin. "You'd have to be pretty stupid to think you were not," she says, "but you have to hide it because if you let on to doctors that you know you are thin, they will want to put weight on you."[9]

4. Lack of menstruation (amenorrhea).
The final major characteristic of anorexia applies only to women who are old enough to menstruate. When a female experiences extreme malnutrition, her reproductive system shuts down, and her period will stop—a condition known as amenorrhea. The *DSM* notes that this condition must continue long enough for the patient to miss at least three menstrual cycles.

The *DSM* guidelines define two different types of anorexia nervosa, the binge-eating/purging type and the restricting type. In the binge-eating/purging type, the individual regularly goes on uncontrolled eating binges followed by efforts to purge, or rid the body of the food consumed, in order to avoid gaining weight. In another variation, the person may

Bingeing and Purging

For many people, eating disorders take the form of uncontrolled eating binges followed by efforts to purge or eliminate the calories consumed. Marya Hornbacher describes the frantic cycle of bingeing and purging in her memoir *Wasted*:

> I stood at the counter, shoveling cereal into my mouth on automatic pilot. I ran out of cereal and moved on to bread, ran out of bread and moved on to eggs, leftovers, ice cream, crackers, stopping every so often to puke in the dark bathroom, staggering back to the kitchen, . . . moving on to the soup my father had made for me to eat over the weekend. I ate all the soup and threw it up, whole noodles and carrots and peas flooding the toilet bowl, spattering the walls, spinning away when I flushed.

By midnight or so, I'd eaten everything in the house except the lime marmalade that had been sitting at the back of the refrigerator for as long as I could remember. I didn't eat the dog food, either. But I thought about it.

Marya Hornbacher. *Wasted: A Memoir of Anorexia and Bulimia.* New York: HarperPerennial, 1999, pp. 220–221.

For many people, eating disorders manifest as uncontrolled eating binges followed by efforts to purge the calories just consumed.

engage in purging without binge eating—that is, they may try to eliminate any food they consumed even though they did not eat an excessive amount in a short period of time. Various methods are used to purge, including self-induced vomiting and misuse of laxatives, diuretics, and enemas. In the restricting type of anorexia nervosa, the affected individual does not engage in bingeing and purging. Instead, his or her weight loss stems from limiting food intake and, in many cases, excessive exercising to burn calories.

Bulimia Nervosa

The *DSM* includes five major characteristics in its definition of bulimia nervosa:

1. Repeated episodes of binge eating.

The ingestion of a large amount of food in a short amount of time is one of the hallmarks of bulimia. This type of bingeing is different from the occasional incident of eating too much and feeling uncomfortably full. Instead, people affected by bulimia feel as if they lack all control over their eating and cannot stop themselves from consuming a huge amount of food. *DSM* defines a binge-eating episode as a period of about two hours or less in which a person eats "an amount of food that is definitely larger than what most people would eat during a similar period of time and under similar circumstances."[10] Often, individuals engaging in bulimic binges will focus on certain types of food that they consider highly fattening. These so-called "bad" foods are typically items that they have tried to avoid as they have become obsessed with their weight.

2. Repeated inappropriate behavior to prevent weight gain.

To avoid gaining weight as a result of their eating binges, people affected by bulimia try to purge the calories consumed by undertaking harmful actions such as self-induced vomiting, fasting, excessive exercise, or the misuse of laxatives, diuretics, enemas, or other medications. Vomiting is by far the most common method of purging, with 80 to 90 percent of bulimia patients indicating that they have engaged in that behavior.

Bulimia nervosa symptoms include an uncontrollable desire to binge on food.

3. Frequent binges and weight-prevention measures.

To meet the *DSM* guidelines for a diagnosis of bulimia, the eating binges and related harmful actions to avoid gaining weight must take place at least twice a week on average and continue over the course of at least two months.

4. Self-evaluation is unduly influenced by body shape and weight.

As is the case with anorexia, people with bulimia are obsessed with their weight and the appearance of their bodies. They allow these factors to play a primary role in determining how they feel about themselves.

5. Disturbance does not occur exclusively during episodes of anorexia nervosa.

Since anorexia and bulimia share several of the same traits, the *DSM* includes this characteristic to prevent misdiagnosis of bulimia. Some people move from one type of eating disorder to another. Most commonly, individuals with anorexia later develop bulimia. One study that looked at anorexia patients over a long period of time found that as many as half of them eventually became bulimic.

According to the *DSM* guidelines, there are two different types of bulimia nervosa, the purging type and the nonpurging type. In the purging type, the affected individual regularly engages in self-induced vomiting or the misuse of laxatives, diuretics, or enemas. In the nonpurging type, the person engages in fasting, excessive exercise, or the misuse of medication in an attempt to compensate for binge eating.

Eating Disorder Not Otherwise Specified

The EDNOS category, as stated in the 2000 *DSM*, "is for disorders of eating that do not meet the criteria for any specific Eating Disorder."[11] In other words, many individuals have an eating disorder but do not meet all of the strict requirements to be diagnosed as having either anorexia or bulimia. The EDNOS category is used to identify and treat such behaviors.

Although the term "eating disorder not otherwise specified" may make these types of behaviors seem less dangerous than anorexia and bulimia, they still can have severe consequences to a person's health and quality of life. In some cases, individuals with EDNOS behaviors are later diagnosed with either anorexia or bulimia as their disorder progresses. EDNOS is also significant because it is the most commonly diagnosed eating disorder.

The list of all the behaviors and conditions that could fall under the EDNOS category is very long. The *DSM* offers a

HEALTH FACT

In a survey of female high school students in the United States, 5.4 percent reported having vomited or taken laxatives to control their weight during the previous thirty days. Among male students, the figure was 2.6 percent.

number of the more common examples, however, which are summarized as follows:

- All of the criteria for anorexia nervosa except that the female sufferer continues to have her period on a regular basis.
- All of the criteria for anorexia nervosa except that the individual's weight remains within the normal range, even though he or she has lost a significant amount of weight.
- All of the criteria for bulimia nervosa cxcept that the binges and compensatory behavior happen less frequently than is specified in the bulimia requirements.
- The affected individual engages in purging or another form of inappropriate behavior even though he or she has not engaged in binge eating. For instance, the person may induce vomiting after eating only a small amount of food.
- The affected individual repeatedly chews large amounts of food but spits it out rather than swallowing it.

Binge-eating disorder (BED) falls under the EDNOS category, but it deserves special attention because it is the most common of the specifically defined disorders. This condition is similar to bulimia, but the binge eating is not accompanied by inappropriate behavior to prevent weight gain. For instance, a person with BED would eat a large amount of food over a short period of time and feel a lack of control over eating, but he or she would not attempt to purge the food, fast, or exercise excessively in response to the binge. Some individuals with BED remain in normal weight ranges. Because people affected by BED do not eliminate the extra calories they consume during eating binges, however, they are frequently overweight or obese.

Physical Effects of Eating Disorders

All types of eating disorders have the potential to cause severe health problems. Many of the effects of eating disorders described below can be found in each of the major disorder categories to varying degrees. In general, people

A Flexible Approach to Diagnosing Eating Disorders

Although the *Diagnostic and Statistical Manual of Mental Disorders* is a valuable tool to help health care professionals diagnose eating disorders, some doctors have criticized its criteria as being too strict—particularly in regard to anorexia nervosa. For instance, critics point out that patients who demonstrate most, but not all, of the major characteristics for anorexia would instead be diagnosed with eating disorder not otherwise specified (EDNOS) if their doctors followed the manual's guidelines to the letter. They argue that many patients in this situation would receive more appropriate treatment if they were diagnosed with anorexia. With this consideration in mind, many doctors employ a flexible approach that uses the *DSM* guidelines as a starting point but also considers the particular circumstances of each individual case in making a diagnosis.

with anorexia tend to experience the most severe health effects because they suffer from malnutrition in addition to other complications. Regardless of the type of eating disorder, however, the risks include both physical harm and mental distress.

In his book *Demystifying Anorexia Nervosa*, Alexander R. Lucas writes that anorexia "is as much a physical disorder as it is a psychiatric one, and certainly the long-term consequences and complications affect the physical health of the individual."[12] The same can be said of the other forms of eating disorders as well. All of the disorders can alter an individual's nutritional intake in extreme ways, and the stresses that purging places on the body can bring other complications.

Starvation is one of the primary threats associated with eating disorders. It is possible for an affected person to consume so little food that they literally starve to death. Although such a dire outcome is by no means common, many sufferers experience severe malnutrition. Malnutrition either causes or contributes to many of the other physical problems described below. It can also greatly complicate the treatment of eating disorders by making it more difficult for

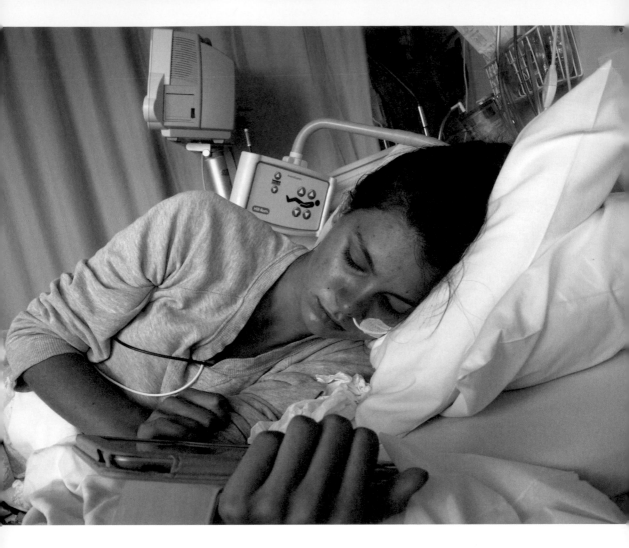

A woman with anorexia receives nutrients through a feeding tube because of her inability to eat properly.

a mental health professional to help a person deal with the emotional issues that underlie the disorder. It is important to remember, however, that not all eating disorders lead to starvation. The condition is most common with anorexia, because one of the primary characteristics of that disorder is extreme weight loss. Individuals with bulimia and EDNOS, on the other hand, may remain close to their normal body weight even though they experience other harmful physical effects of their eating disorder.

Heart-related problems are another serious concern for people affected by eating disorders. When an individual is deprived of sufficient nutrition for an extended period of time, his or her heart can weaken to the point that it is unable to circulate blood properly. Purging, through repeated vomiting or the use of medications to eliminate food, can also cause damage to the heart. People with weakened hearts frequently feel cold, particularly in their hands and feet, because there is a lack of sufficient blood flow to keep all parts of the body warm. People affected by eating disorders often develop other serious issues related to the heart, including an irregular heartbeat (known as arrhythmia), a slow heart rate (measuring less than fifty beats per minute), heart murmurs (caused by problems with valves in the heart), and low blood pressure. These issues may restrict blood flow to the brain, causing dizziness and fainting, or to other parts of the body, causing tissue damage. Most dangerous of all, these heart-related problems place individuals at greater risk of heart attack or heart stoppage, both of which can be fatal.

Cognitive problems can also result from eating disorders. Extended malnutrition can inhibit the functioning of the brain and slow thinking processes. It can also contribute to psychological and behavioral issues, such as obsessive-compulsive disorder, anxiety, and depression.

Blood problems are another common side effect of eating disorders. A lack of proper nutrition, as well as the harmful effects of purging, can change the level of electrolytes (salts) in the bloodstream. Electrolyte imbalances can contribute to some of the heart problems mentioned above as well as increase the likelihood of seizures. Changes in electrolyte levels can also alter the production of blood cells and platelets, resulting in such symptoms as fatigue, pale complexion, excessive bruising, and bleeding in the nose or gums. Finally, malnutrition and electrolyte problems can create a shortage of white blood cells. Such shortages can make an individual more vulnerable to infections.

Hormonal and reproductive problems often result from eating disorders as well. A lack of proper nutrition and the process of purging can interfere with the release of key hormones, including estrogen in females and testosterone in males. This disturbance can affect physical growth for individuals who have not reached adulthood, and the

Anorexia Affects Your Whole Body

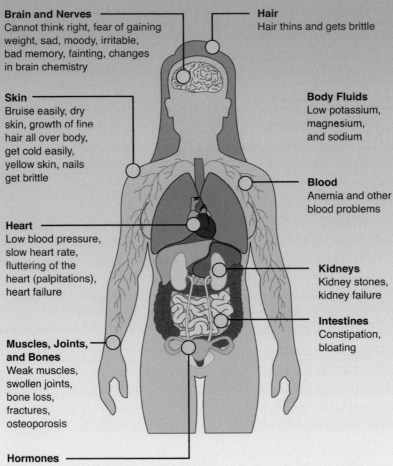

Brain and Nerves
Cannot think right, fear of gaining weight, sad, moody, irritable, bad memory, fainting, changes in brain chemistry

Hair
Hair thins and gets brittle

Skin
Bruise easily, dry skin, growth of fine hair all over body, get cold easily, yellow skin, nails get brittle

Body Fluids
Low potassium, magnesium, and sodium

Blood
Anemia and other blood problems

Heart
Low blood pressure, slow heart rate, fluttering of the heart (palpitations), heart failure

Kidneys
Kidney stones, kidney failure

Intestines
Constipation, bloating

Muscles, Joints, and Bones
Weak muscles, swollen joints, bone loss, fractures, osteoporosis

Hormones
Periods stop, problems growing, trouble getting pregnant. If pregnant, higher risk for miscarriage, having a Cesarean section, baby with low birthweight, and postpartum depression.

Taken from: Women'sHealth.gov. Anorexia Fact Sheet, p. 3. http://womenshealth.gov/publications/fact-sheet /anorexia-nervosa.cfm.

changes that come with puberty may slow down or stop. Women who had previously been menstruating may experience amenorrhea, which means that they will be unable to become pregnant as long as that condition persists. There is also evidence that anorexia can cause long-term damage to the reproductive system, possibly creating fertility problems even after a woman recovers from the disorder. Males affected by eating disorders may also face fertility issues as a result of hormonal changes.

Bone problems are another common physical effect of eating disorders. The diets of malnourished individuals often lack key minerals, such as calcium. Combined with disturbances in the release of hormones, diminished intake of important nutrients prevents bones from developing properly. The result is osteoporosis, or loss of bone density. Although this condition is serious at any time in life, it is especially so in children and adolescents. If an eating disorder persists long enough among members of these age groups, nonreversible bone loss and permanent stunting of growth can be the result. In addition, individuals with osteoporosis face a greater risk of breaking bones.

Dental and digestive problems often arise due to the direct effect of eating disorders on all parts of the body related to the consumption and digestion of food. Purging can be harmful in many ways. The process of vomiting brings

A healthy dorsal vertebra, left, and one affected by osteoporosis, showing the decrease in bone density. People with anorexia often develop osteoporosis from lack of nutrition.

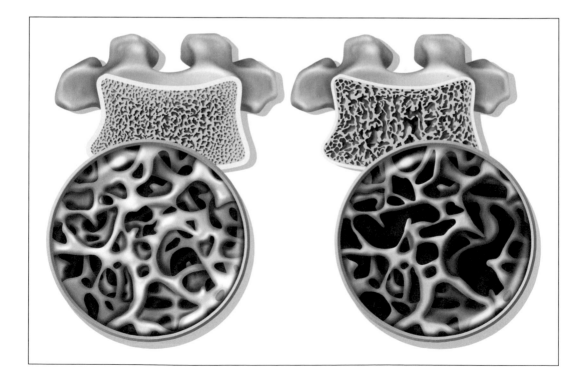

stomach acids into contact with the mouth and teeth. These acids are highly corrosive and can cause tooth erosion, which is one of the early signs that doctors use to identify patients with eating disorders that involve purging. In addition, the physical process of inducing vomiting and repeated contact with stomach acids can irritate the lining of the mouth, esophagus, and stomach, which in some instances can cause life-threatening bleeding. Regular purging with laxatives can result in constipation when no laxatives are taken, which in turn can cause intestinal problems. Finally, starvation can slow down and interrupt the digestive process, which can impair the functioning of the liver.

Eating disorders can affect other parts of the body as well. Inadequate intake of vitamins, minerals, and fats can cause dry, flaky skin and thin, brittle hair. In certain cases, a downy type of hair known as lanugo may grow on the body as a means of preserving heat.

Finally, significant changes in a person's energy level sometimes accompany malnutrition. In some cases, affected individuals become very lethargic and sleep a great deal to compensate for the body's depleted energy reserves. In other cases, the opposite occurs and individuals display highly energetic, upbeat, or even hyperactive behavior. This phenomenon stems from the fact that severe dietary deficiencies can release endorphins, a chemical in the brain that for some people produces a feeling that is similar to being under the influence of a stimulant. "Intense hunger acted on me like a double espresso," recalls Ilana Kurshan. "I was wired, energized, alert and intensely charged. I found myself unable to ever stand still: I'd run to and from my classes instead of shuffling along with the crowds."[13]

Psychological Effects of Eating Disorders

Though eating disorders are themselves classified as psychological or mental health disorders, they are often associated with other emotional, behavioral, and psychological ailments, including depression, anxiety disorder, obsessive-compulsive disorder, and bipolar disorder.

A Colorless World

Eating disorders are associated with a wide range of health effects, both physical and mental, that can make life very difficult for individuals affected by them. In the following passage from her book *The Long Road Back,* Judy Tam Sargent describes the misery she endured during her battle with anorexia.

An anorexic person in the throes of an illness will never tell you this, but I can tell you from my own experience: living with anorexia on a daily basis is miserable. Worse than my depression or my obsessive thoughts and compulsions were the physical effects of my state of starvation.

I was always cold—so cold that my lips and fingernails stayed blue even in the summertime, even with several layers of clothing. The word "cold" takes on a new meaning when you're anorexic. It's a chilled-to-the-bone kind of cold. I have never been cold to the same extent since my recovery.

Starved of nutrients, my brain went haywire. All my waking moments were filled with disturbing thoughts. I was never insane or psychotic, but I often felt as if I were. . . .

I was always tired, even after sleeping for long periods. Getting myself out of bed became increasingly difficult. . . . The world had lost all its color, and life had lost all its joy and meaning.

Judy Tam Sargent. *The Long Road Back: A Survivor's Guide to Anorexia.* Georgetown, MA: North Star, 1999, p. 84.

Health researchers estimate that these types of conditions affect 70 percent of people with anorexia and 75 percent of people with bulimia. Neurotic symptoms such as guilt, anxiety, and nervous tension are particularly common in individuals with bulimia. That disorder is also associated

Individuals with eating disorders are often tired and may find it difficult to get out of bed.

with risky behavior such as substance abuse, stealing, and sexual promiscuity. Moreover, traits such as perfectionism and low self-esteem are commonly found among people affected by various forms of eating disorders.

The fact that eating disorders and other psychological disorders often appear together has raised questions about the nature of the relationship between the ailments. Are eating disorders in some sense caused by other disorders, or are the other disorders caused by eating disorders? The issue is a complicated one, and the answers are not completely clear. Researchers have not been able to identify one type of disorder as the reason that another developed. As a result, when such coinciding ailments are present, doctors generally believe that neither is secondary to the other. Instead, they view them as separate disorders that may be related to and reinforce one another.

Eating disorders also contribute to potentially deadly psychological stress. A 2008 study found that nearly 17 percent of people with anorexia attempted suicide at one time or another, and that number was even higher for those with the bingeing and purging form of the disorder. Other researchers have publicized similar findings for people with bulimia. The risk of suicide among all eating-disorder patients increases greatly when the individual also suffers from depression.

Eating Disorders and Mortality

Eating disorders can have severe effects on an individual's health, and in extreme cases can even cause death. The mortality rates vary considerably among the different disorders. Anorexia is by far the most dangerous and, in fact, ranks among the most deadly of all psychological disorders. Its mortality rate has been estimated at 5.6 percent per decade, with most deaths resulting from starvation, heart or gastrointestinal problems, infection, and suicide. Research has also shown that anorexia drastically impacts life expectancy. A patient who develops the disorder at age fifteen lives an average of twenty-five fewer years than someone without anorexia. Bulimia and EDNOS are far less likely to cause death, though individuals with these disorders often face severe physical and mental complications. In addition, suicide can be a serious concern for people with these ailments.

CHAPTER 3

Causes and Risk Factors

Eating disorders often develop quite suddenly and with little advance warning. When an individual is first diagnosed with an eating disorder, his or her loved ones are often left wondering, "How did this happen?" "It's a scary thing for parents when eight months before you've got a seemingly normal child and then you find her in the adult psychiatric unit," one mother explains in *Inside Anorexia: The Experiences of Girls and Their Families.* "It's terribly frightening for a sixteen-year-old who just thinks she's only got a problem with eating. She doesn't really quite understand that it's a mental illness too. That was incredibly difficult for us. . . . It was just a horrible, horrible experience."[14]

The truth is that no one knows for certain what causes eating disorders. Unlike many physical diseases, the underlying causes of psychological illnesses are difficult to trace, and theories about their origins are difficult to prove. The source of each person's ailment can be highly individualized, shaped by countless different influences in their lives and by the unique aspects of their personality and behavior.

Most health experts believe that eating disorders develop through a complex interaction between various elements. These elements may include the environment people live in, their personal reactions to the stresses in their lives, and genetic traits they have inherited. As a result, medical professionals do not usually focus on identifying a specific cause for eating disorders, but instead highlight numerous risk factors related to the disease. Experiencing one or even several of these risk factors does not automatically mean that an individual will develop an eating disorder. Under certain circumstances, however, the conditions detailed below can play a role in the development of an eating disorder.

Researchers estimate that 90 percent of those affected by eating disorders are female, which means that girls and women are at substantially greater risk of developing eating disorders than boys and men. A variety of factors may contribute to this phenomenon. For instance, the social and cultural

Traditional gender roles may make females more susceptible to feelings of low self-esteem and a lack of control over their lives. These feelings may contribute to the development of an eating disorder in certain individuals.

pressure to strive for a certain ideal of physical appearance often focuses more strongly on females than on males. This pressure is particularly strong during adolescence, and the anxiety that some girls feel about their physical appearance during this period is made worse by the fact that their bodies are going through significant changes.

In addition, traditional gender roles may make females more susceptible to feelings of low self-esteem and a perceived lack of control over their lives, and they may develop disordered eating behavior as a response to such thinking. Genetics, too, may play a role. It is possible that biological differences may make females more susceptible to eating disorders, though there have been no conclusive findings on this front. While gender is considered a risk factor, however, it is important to remember that eating disorders affect both men and women, and that the number of cases among males may be higher than estimated.

Unhealthy Dieting in a World Where Thinness Is Prized

The Western countries where eating disorders are most common tend to place a strong cultural emphasis on the value of being slender. That ideal is continually reinforced in popular media outlets. From commercials that tout diet products to the extremely thin models featured in fashion advertisements, the public is bombarded with the message that having low body weight is a key to happiness, success, and fame.

Not everyone accepts this superficial notion, of course, but the prevalence of this cultural message may encourage susceptible individuals to pursue weight loss by any means. Writer Jennifer Egan describes the importance of this cultural influence in the development of her disordered eating behavior as a young teen: "I began to soothe myself with fantasies, visions in which I became popular, irresistible, strong like the models in my mother's fashion magazines (which I devoured); visions in which I was searingly, mightily, unstoppably thin. [A magazine] article on anorexia, intended as a cautionary tale, functioned for me as a how-to manual."[15]

Many individuals who later develop an eating disorder first undertake a diet in an attempt to lose weight. Dieting is extremely widespread, and it is not necessarily dangerous provided that it is undertaken in a healthy manner. In some cases, however, their efforts to shed pounds lead dieters to unhealthy actions such as skipping meals, abusing laxatives, and inducing vomiting. If such behavior becomes a habit, a full-blown eating disorder can develop. It is important to note, though, that eating disorders are not simply "diets gone wrong." They are complex psychological disorders that are usually fueled by many underlying factors. As a result, recovery is not as simple as ending a diet and restoring previous eating patterns.

Exercise can figure into eating disorders as well. Exercise itself is not harmful, of course, and it is usually considered part of a healthy lifestyle. The problem arises when an individual engages in excessive exercise that becomes an unrelenting obsession. Such behavior may be a sign of a dangerous fixation on weight and body image that can contribute to the development of an eating disorder.

In addition, women who pursue athletics at an elite level can develop a particular type of condition known as female athlete triad, which results from a desire to lose weight to improve performance in a particular sport. The three elements that make up the triad are disordered eating; amenorrhea, or loss of period; and osteoporosis, or bone loss. In many cases, individuals affected by female athlete triad could also be diagnosed with anorexia, bulimia, or EDNOS, depending on their particular behavior and symptoms.

Puberty, Adolescence, and Anxiety About Growing Up

The period when eating disorders most frequently appear extends from the onset of puberty through early adulthood. The physical, emotional, and social changes that accompany

"I Didn't Want to Be a Woman"

Feelings of anxiety about growing up can play a significant role in the development of eating disorders. In the passage below from her book *The Art of Starvation,* Sheila MacLeod describes the feelings of fear and hopelessness that drove her toward anorexia.

When I began not to eat it was out of apathy and depression, out of a hopelessness concerning myself (including my body), rather than according to a definite plan.

The inescapable fact is that I didn't want to be a woman, although I was unaware of this at the time. What I did know is that I didn't want to grow up. . . . To me, the adult world was not a place where the individual could act freely and achieve growth, both in the acceptance of responsibility and in the likelihood of success. To me, it was just another place where I would be pushed around, perhaps even more violently than I had been before.

Sheila MacLeod. *The Art of Starvation*. London: Virago, 1981, p. 70.

that stage of life can contribute to the development of eating disorders. For females, the physical changes associated with puberty—including the beginning of their menstrual cycle, changes in body shape, and an increase in body weight—can heighten girls' self-consciousness and provoke worries about appearance. Moreover, both males and females become increasingly concerned about physical attractiveness and romantic relationships at this stage. All of these elements can trigger a strong desire to lose weight, which has the potential to cause disordered eating behavior and to inspire an excessive exercise regimen. Adolescence is also a time when individuals face new responsibilities and pressures and become more aware of the challenges that they will be required to take on as adults. This increased awareness can provoke severe anxiety about growing up, and some individuals may develop disordered eating behavior in response.

Psychologists have noted that eating disorders sometimes stem from a person's desire to exert control over his or her life. Such feelings can be closely related to the stress that comes with adolescence, though they can also develop from other factors. For individuals with these types of worries, an eating disorder can provide a form of reassurance. It offers them an opportunity to carefully arrange at least one element of their existence—their diet. "Looking back, it is easy for me to recognize my own intense need for control and order and to see how that need expressed itself in my relationship to food," explains John Nolan, who developed anorexia nervosa at age twelve. "I tried to exert control over my body as a way of feeling in control of other aspects of my life."[16]

Experts who analyze eating disorders from a feminist perspective often place a strong emphasis on the role that a desire for control plays in the development of the disorders. According to this school of thought, the inequality experienced by women in society can make them feel as if they have very little authority over their lives. For some women, eating disorders may be a response to this sense of powerlessness.

Personality and Psychological Factors

Certain personality traits and psychological conditions are frequently associated with eating disorders. Therefore, individuals who demonstrate these behaviors are thought to be at greater risk of developing an eating disorder. In some cases, a person may be affected by a definite psychological disorder that is recognized as separate from his or her problems related to eating. These conditions can include mood disorders, such as bipolar disorder and depression; anxiety disorders, such as obsessive-compulsive disorder; and substance abuse disorders, including alcoholism and drug addiction.

Other psychological characteristics and personality traits are also common among people affected by eating disorders, though these traits may be less apparent than those that make up a diagnosable psychological illness. Nonetheless, these characteristics are notable because their presence may indicate that a person is more susceptible to developing an eating disorder. In addition, they often play a role in the specific actions that a person with an eating disorder takes with regard to food and eating.

Perfectionism can contribute to all types of eating disorders but seems to play a particularly significant role in anorexia. People with a tendency toward perfectionism

Some eating disorder patients may also be affected by other psychological disorders, such as bipolar disorder.

believe that they must complete every task they undertake flawlessly, and they wish to be recognized as superior in whatever they do. Whenever they fall short of that impossible goal, they experience great stress. When the perfectionist mentality is applied to the goal of weight loss, such individuals often come to believe that they can never be thin enough. Their unbending determination to lose more weight can lead to extreme results. "I always wanted to do well in everything I did," notes one anorexia patient, "so I had to do well at being anorexic. When I first got sick, I had to be the *best anorexic*. I would compete against all the other anorexic patients."[17]

Low self-esteem also seems to play a role in many eating disorders. People with low self-esteem believe that they are unworthy in some way or lack some essential quality. They feel dissatisfied with their lives and discouraged about their prospects for the future. For such individuals, the idea of losing weight can be attractive as a means of feeling better about themselves. If disordered eating behavior takes hold, however, it can do further harm to the individuals' self-esteem. This is particularly true for people who engage in bingeing, as each episode of excessive eating can make them doubt their self-worth to an even greater degree. These thoughts, in turn, can inspire them to take dangerous actions to compensate for the calories consumed during the binge. "After a while, feelings of inadequacy would lead me to binge," remembers one former bulimia patient, "which would lead me to more feelings of inadequacy and then throwing up, and all of it just became such a cycle, . . . hating myself so I didn't wanna see people, and then hating myself 'cause I didn't have friends. . . . And it was all so connected, it just all fed on itself."[18]

Obsessive behavior involves an overwhelming fixation on particular objects or actions. Excessive and repeated hand washing is one example of obsessive behavior. If such thoughts become especially urgent and all-encompassing, a person may be diagnosed with obsessive-compulsive disorder (OCD). While obsessive behavior can be directed toward many different actions, for those who develop eating disorders it is often focused on food and various aspects of the eating process. This is true even for people affected by eating disorders who are determined to eat as little as possible and seem to go to great lengths to avoid food. For instance, it is not unusual for an individual with anorexia to take great delight in preparing a meal, even though he or she consumes almost none of it.

HEALTH FACT

Anorexia is among the most deadly of all psychological disorders.

One example of obsessive-compulsive behavior is an excessive washing of the hands.

The obsessive behavior of people with eating disorders can also be seen in their often strict dining habits. For instance, some people establish elaborate rituals in which they eat the same food at the same time each day. Any variation in that routine can be a source of great psychological stress. As a result, many people with eating disorders avoid get-togethers that involve food, because such events place them at risk of revealing or varying their eating practices.

Linkages Between Traumatic Events and Eating Disorders

Many people who receive treatment for an eating disorder indicate that they previously experienced some type of traumatic or stressful event in their lives. Some experts believe that such events can contribute to the development of eating disorders. For many years, experts tended to place a strong emphasis on sexual abuse as a possible cause of eating disorders, but the results of scientific studies have shown that it may not have as large an influence as was once thought. An analysis conducted in the 1990s of various research studies on the subject indicated that around 30 percent of people affected by eating disorders had a history of sexual abuse. While this figure is somewhat higher than the prevalence of sexual abuse in the general population, which is thought to be around 20 percent, it also indicates that the majority of people with eating disorders do not have a history of sexual abuse.

Overall, abuse of any kind—sexual, physical, or emotional—can be considered a risk factor for the development of an eating disorder, but it would be wrong to think that most people with eating disorders have been abused. If bulimia is considered by itself, however, abuse seems to be a more common element. One study found that more than half of those who were bulimic had been raped, molested, or physically assaulted.

Abuse of any kind, be it emotional, sexual, or physical, is a risk factor for the development of an eating disorder.

Feelings and Frayed Wires

Experts believe that a wide variety of factors may contribute to the development of eating disorders. Many of these factors are psychological or emotional, rather than physical, in nature. "Eating disorders, then, are not really about food," Carrie Arnold writes in *Next to Nothing: A Firsthand Account of One Teenager's Experience with an Eating Disorder*.

> They are about how you feel about yourself; they are about low self-esteem, a tremendous need to feel in control of yourself and your surroundings, unrelenting perfectionism, and an alienation of the mind from the body. They are also about a brain gone awry, frayed wires sparking and igniting as the brain is unable to process messages about food and anxiety normally.

Carrie Arnold, with Timothy B. Walsh, MD. *Next to Nothing: A Firsthand Account of One Teenager's Experience with an Eating Disorder*. New York: Oxford University Press, 2007, p. 6.

Few studies have been undertaken to explore possible linkages between eating disorders and potentially traumatic life events, such as enrolling in a new school, moving away from home for the first time, attending a summer camp, being teased about weight or appearance, or breaking up with a boyfriend or girlfriend. Some research, however, has suggested that individuals who experienced a death in the family or a significant separation from their loved ones have a slightly increased chance of developing bulimia.

Significant life events do seem to figure prominently in the accounts that eating-disorder patients give of their experiences. Many people report that their disordered eating behavior began or intensified shortly after they encountered some new stress in their lives. For example, Lisa Himmel recounts how her bulimia developed shortly after she started college:

I was just not ready to leave home and go to college. I clung to the guidance of my parents, but they weren't there supplying me with fresh groceries, nor did I have someone to accommodate my specific dietary requests. . . . I was always hungry, and being a hungry freshman in college, a foreigner on new ground, blew out my tightly controlled system. I binged, at first not frequently, maybe once or twice a week and always on Fridays. I started throwing up to alleviate the pain of being full.[19]

Family Relationships and Heredity

In seeking explanations for various types of mental disorders, psychologists often analyze the relationships within a patient's family. Eating disorders are no exception. Some studies have found that eating-disorder patients have frequently experienced significant levels of unhappiness or discomfort with family dynamics—and parent-child relationships in particular. Researchers say, for example, that the pressure of pleasing overprotective or demanding parents can sometimes contribute to the development of eating disorders in young adults.

The issue of conflict avoidance can also figure into the development of eating disorders. A family's inability to discuss issues or deal with problems creates stress in the home, and a young person's disordered eating may be an unconscious effort to resolve the situation. Finally, some individuals with an eating disorder report that one or both of their parents suffer from psychological difficulties of their own.

The last risk factor that may contribute to the development of eating disorders is heredity, or genetics. Unlike other explanations that focus on psychological or environmental factors, this one suggests that physical factors—the genes they inherit or specific elements in their body chemistry—may make certain people more likely to develop an eating disorder than others. The belief that genetics may play a role in eating disorders is based on research studies that have analyzed eating disorders within families. These studies indicate that when one member of a family develops an eating

According to studies, it is much more likely that both members of a set of identical twins will develop anorexia than both members of a set of fraternal twins.

disorder, the other members of that family have a substantially greater risk of developing the same disorder, as compared with members of the general population.

Other studies have looked at the differences between identical twins (who have the exact same genetic code, or DNA) and fraternal twins (who only share about half of their DNA, like any other siblings). According to these studies, it is much more likely that both members of a set of identical twins will develop anorexia than both members of a set of fraternal twins. This finding may indicate that genetic factors influence anorexia to some degree, though the impact seems to be minimal with regard to bulimia.

Another area of study involves the chemical neurotransmitters that are part of the human brain. Some medical researchers have suggested that disordered eating—both restricting food and bingeing—may be the result of problems with chemicals in the brain that regulate feelings of hunger and fullness. According to this theory, when those chemicals do not work properly, a person lacks the normal triggers that tell the body when to eat and when to stop eating.

Although a growing amount of research has been focused on the role of genetics and brain chemistry in eating disorders, the results have thus far been inconclusive. Some experts have even criticized this area of study. They believe that genetics are a relatively minor factor in eating disorders. Critics point out that shifts in genetic predispositions for illness are thought to occur gradually over a long period of time, yet eating disorders seem to have increased significantly in the span of just a few decades.

Health care professionals who believe that genetics and biology play an important role in eating disorders offer an explanation for these findings. They argue that while a person's DNA may make him or her more susceptible to developing an eating disorder, it takes other, outside influences to touch off the disordered behavior. According to one analogy, genetics "loads the gun" for someone to develop an eating disorder, but a combination of factors in the individual's environment or lifestyle serves to "pull the trigger."

CHAPTER 4

Treatment of Eating Disorders

Many individuals who are deeply caught up in an eating disorder find it difficult even to consider the subject of treatment. Most feel panicked at the prospect of regular eating, which is one of the essential actions they need to take to get better. Recovery from eating disorders can also be greatly complicated by the impaired thinking that results from malnutrition, and by underlying psychological conditions such as depression and severe anxiety. In addition, people with eating disorders may avoid seeking treatment because they believe that it will just be too difficult. "Treatment is work," Marianne Apostolides acknowledges in her memoir *Inner Hunger: A Young Woman's Struggle Through Anorexia and Bulimia.* "I don't want to underplay the slow, difficult, and frustrating nature of treatment, because I don't want you to quit before you have gotten what you need. So I am urging you to hold onto the knowledge that although treatment is arduous, it is your one path to freedom."[20]

Since recovery is so difficult, most people with eating disorders require outside assistance to get better. In many cases, treatment begins only after someone else intervenes. A parent may discover evidence that her child is purging, for instance, or a teacher or coach may notice signs of fatigue in a student. Similarly, a friend may become concerned about extreme shifts in behavior or excessive weight loss.

However the intervention takes place, the key is to convince the person affected by an eating disorder to seek professional help as soon as possible. Studies have shown that patients have a better chance of recovery if their disorders have not continued for an extended period of time. The treatment process can begin with a visit to a family doctor or, if necessary, a hospital emergency room. Many patients, however, ultimately receive the majority of their care from a doctor or facility that specializes in eating disorders.

Early treatment can greatly increase a patient's chances of overcoming an eating disorder.

Initial Assessment

As a first step, doctors typically perform a comprehensive physical exam to determine the patient's condition. If they diagnose critical medical problems, they may recommend immediate hospitalization. This precaution is most common among individuals with anorexia nervosa who are suffering the extreme effects of starvation, or any patient with an eating disorder who has developed dangerous complications related to their blood, heart, or other vital organs.

Interviews and psychological assessments play an important role in the treatment of eating disorders.

An early priority in treatment involves taking steps to counteract the malnutrition experienced by those who have severely restricted their diet. This step is necessary not only to improve the patient's physical health, but also because hunger can strongly affect how the mind works. Once adequate nutrition is restored, the patient will be better equipped to respond positively to additional treatment.

A Weight-Gain Trick

People affected by eating disorders often have an intense fear of gaining weight. This fear may push them to extreme lengths to avoid eating, even after they enter a treatment program. In her book *The Long Road Back*, Judy Tam Sargent remembers engaging in elaborate deceptions in order to convince the hospital staff that she was conquering anorexia. "I knew the staff wanted me to gain weight, so I gained weight for them," she writes.

> But it was artificial weight. As soon as I caught on to what I needed to do, I spent a week playing the hospital's game by drinking progressively greater amounts of water before my morning weigh-ins. I had an alarm clock, and I knew when they'd be coming to weigh me. Two eight-ounce cups of water weigh a pound [0.4L]; it's a matter of simple mathematics. Near the end of my stay, I was drinking as much as twenty cups of water each morning. . . . My weight gain pleased the staff, and that was what mattered. Nobody thought to question the fact that I was gaining weight despite my continual refusal to eat. I was discharged from the hospital.

Judy Tam Sargent. *The Long Road Back: A Survivor's Guide to Anorexia*. Georgetown, MA: North Star, 1999, pp. 28–29.

Deceptive tricks such as drinking an excessive amount of water are used by some eating disorder patients to cheat on their weight gain goals.

To help gain a better understanding of the patient's behavior and the underlying factors that may be contributing to the disorder, doctors conduct interviews and psychological assessments that have been specifically designed to diagnose eating disorders. At this point—if not before—a crucial aspect of treatment becomes clear. Many patients will not be honest about their condition and their disordered behavior, either out of shame or a genuine conviction that their eating behavior is necessary to ward off unwanted weight gain. In fact, it is not unusual for patients to resist any help that is offered to them for an extended period of time. People with eating disorders often try to deceive the medical staff, evade the diet plan that is established for them, and purge in secret.

To help get around this obstacle, many eating-disorder specialists attempt to take the focus off of eating and weight gain during the interview process. For instance, they may initially ask more open-ended questions about the person's feelings and the problems in his or her life. As treatment progresses, though, the medical staff will try to convince the patient to accept the fact that he or she has a serious disorder. Admitting that a problem exists is an essential step in moving toward recovery.

Treatment Environments

Once the primary assessment is completed, the doctor, patient, and family members need to agree on a course of action. One of the first agenda items is to select a treatment location and program. These choices are frequently dictated by the severity of the patient's condition, but factors ranging from ease of transportation to health insurance coverage can play a role as well. It is not unusual for an individual patient to experience several different treatment approaches, beginning with a closely supervised environment and moving toward more independent methods, as they make progress in combating the disorder. Some of the most common approaches are described below.

Inpatient hospitalization is the most restrictive type of treatment. It involves admission to a hospital ward, where the individual receives any necessary medical treatment and takes part in psychological therapy. One of the biggest advantages to inpatient care is that it allows the hospital staff to closely monitor the patient's diet, behavior, and weight. Such close supervision helps the staff to keep track of whether the patient follows the prescribed meal plan and whether he or she attempts to purge the food consumed. Inpatient care is usually the best choice in cases where the individual's medical condition is poor, the disordered behavior is severe, the patient seems likely to evade treatment, or the patient is considered at risk for suicide.

Residential treatment provides many of the same features as inpatient hospitalization, but the care facility typically seems more like a home environment and less like a hospital. Because they cannot provide all the medical resources that a hospital can, residential treatment facilities usually do not admit patients whose medical condition is unstable. In addition to offering psychological counseling and diet supervision, residential treatment centers often focus on therapy

A woman with anorexia is counseled as she eats at a treatment facility.

Mealtime in the Clinic

The physical treatment for eating disorders often involves putting patients on a special diet aimed at helping them gain weight. In the following excerpt from *Teens with Eating Disorders,* one young woman recalls her experiences with eating at a residential treatment facility. "We had a separate room for eating meals," she says.

> We all sat around a table, all the girls in our unit, and our trays would be in front of us. We had half an hour for meals and fifteen minutes for snacks. It was horrible—just horrible. It seemed like we were always eating. I understand that they were trying to build our weight back up, but my gosh, I felt like every ten minutes they were sitting a tray down in front of me. And they supervised every meal, every snack. . . . You had to eat, you had to. If you didn't, they'd make you drink a supplement to make up the calories. The supplement was this liquid stuff that tasted horrible, and no one wanted to have it. So we ate.

Quoted in Gail B. Stewart. *Teens with Eating Disorders.* San Diego: Lucent, 2001, p. 99.

that involves group activities and creative outlets such as art and music. They also provide opportunities for patients to travel to off-site locations so that they can gain experience in managing their disorder in the types of real-world settings they will face when they leave the residential facility.

Day hospital treatment is a less-intensive option that allows patients to continue living in the community, either on their own or with their family. Patients attend a supervised treatment program at a hospital facility for a set amount of time each day, usually three to five hours. Although this arrangement provides structured care and close supervision, it also makes it easier for patients to continue with their school studies or work commitments. Like residential treatment facilities, day hospital programs are not considered appropriate for patients whose medical condition is unstable.

Outpatient treatment is an even less-intensive method in which patients attend regular counseling or group therapy sessions. Since health care providers cannot actively monitor eating behavior in an outpatient setting, the patient and his or her family are responsible for maintaining a prescribed diet plan and avoiding unhealthy actions such as purging and excessive exercise.

In most of the environments mentioned above, the patient works closely with a team of people who are responsible for two different aspects of treatment: physical and psychological. A dietitian typically oversees the physical process of recovery from an eating disorder. Dietitians are medical professionals who specialize in nutrition and healthy eating. Dietitians help patients to reestablish healthy eating patterns and, when necessary, to gain weight. The dietitian develops a diet plan that provides balanced nutrition with sufficient calories to reach the weight goal that has been established for each patient. This process can be a struggle for all concerned, as most people who receive treatment for eating disorders are highly resistant to eating. Many patients are initially appalled by the amount of food they are asked to consume. In fact, some patients will try to cling to a restricted diet by claiming to be allergic to certain foods, although their supposed allergies are often invented as an effort to avoid foods that they perceive as fattening.

Treating the emotional and behavioral aspects of eating disorders is usually handled by psychotherapists. These mental health professionals are responsible for evaluating the patient's psychological condition. The therapist's job is to help the patient understand and come to terms with factors that may have contributed to the development of his or her eating disorder. The therapist also assists the individual in finding ways to manage stress without resorting to harmful behavior.

Psychotherapy

The word *psychotherapy* typically conjures up images of one-on-one sessions with a psychologist in which the patient confesses intimate personal details of his or her life. In truth, individual sessions with a therapist often do play a part in the treatment process for eating disorders. A patient may also participate in a variety of other activities, though, including group meetings and discussions that include family members. The methods that psychotherapists use in treating eating disorders can vary greatly, depending on their training and professional philosophy. Some practitioners and treatment facilities specialize in specific types of treatment, while others offer a mixed approach that draws on several different kinds of therapy.

Two forms of therapy, in particular, have received a great deal of attention because of their effectiveness in treating eating disorders: the Maudsley method and cognitive behavioral therapy. The Maudsley method is the best known of the several different types of family therapy. Although it is primarily used for patients with anorexia nervosa, it has also been applied to other eating disorders. Cognitive behavioral therapy is also used to treat many types of eating disorders, but it has proven to be especially effective for bulimia nervosa and binge-eating disorder.

The Maudsley method takes its name from the hospital in London, England, where it was first developed. The central component of this therapy is the active involvement of the patient's family in treating the eating disorder. Parents and siblings attend counseling sessions with the patient, and they play an important role in each stage of the therapy, which usually takes place over twelve months on an outpatient basis.

When used to treat anorexia, the Maudsley method begins with a refeeding process in which the family helps the patient to gain weight and adopt healthy and consistent eating behaviors. The family members are responsible for designing and carrying out the meal plan, though they receive guidance from a therapist and a dietitian. The second phase of treatment includes further counseling about anorexia, as well as advice on how to manage social situations and activities that can trigger disordered behavior. The final phase begins after the patient reaches and maintains an appropriate weight. At that point, the therapy concentrates on improving relations among the family members, providing them with problem-solving skills,

and helping them to establish and maintain a supportive environment.

The Maudsley method requires great determination from the patient's family members. Their commitment to the process is particularly important during the refeeding phase, when the patient is likely to be very resistant to eating. "At the worst times, we had to isolate our younger children to keep them safe because Chloe would hurl things around," remembers one woman who treated her daughter at home with the Maudsley method. "One time our toddler was running by and a dinner plate narrowly missed her head. . . . And the children could hear—the whole street could hear—Chloe's screaming and shouting."[21]

The second method of treatment for eating disorders, cognitive behavioral therapy (CBT), has been the subject of numerous medical studies since the early 1990s. The results have been so encouraging that many specialists consider CBT to be "the treatment of choice"[22] for bulimia nervosa, according

The Maudsley method uses the family to help the patient adopt healthy and consistent eating behavior.

to Carlos M. Grilo in his book *Eating and Weight Disorders*. It is also widely considered to be one of the best options for helping individuals with binge-eating disorder, and it is used to treat other disorders as well.

When applied to bulimia, CBT focuses on the destructive cycle of behavior experienced by affected individuals. That cycle often begins with feelings of unhappiness and low self-esteem. To cope with these feelings, the individual tries to lose weight. Efforts at weight loss lead to extreme dieting, and then to bingeing and purging. This behavior, in turn, creates more negative feelings, which causes the cycle to start anew.

CBT addresses the bulimia cycle with a three-stage approach. It usually takes place over a four-month period and can be applied on an individual or group basis. In the first stage, patients receive education about the nature of the disorder and learn the importance of establishing a regular, healthy pattern of eating. The main idea in this stage is to convince patients to abandon not only their restrictive diet, but also the bingeing and purging that follows. To help achieve that end, patients maintain a detailed daily record of what they eat and their feelings about food. This food journal remains a central tool through-out the treatment process.

In stage two of the CBT approach, psychotherapists help patients expand their diet so that they learn to responsibly consume some of the "bad" foods that were part of their binges. They also challenge the dysfunctional beliefs and perceptions patients have about eating, weight, and self-image, and teach them problem-solving skills that will help them deal with difficulties in a constructive manner. Finally, in stage three

HEALTH FACT

For a person suffering the effects of starvation, consuming too much food can be harmful or even deadly. The chemically depleted cells in the body cannot keep up with the sudden boost in metabolism when the person starts eating, and the resulting drop in blood plasma levels can cause the person to experience a seizure, lapse into a coma, or suffer heart failure. To avoid this danger, health care professionals use a very gradual approach when helping patients with eating disorders increase their weight.

In the first stage of cognitive behavior therapy, patients receive education about the nature of their disorder and learn the importance of establishing a regular pattern of healthy eating.

psychotherapists teach patients how to identify and cope with high-stress situations and how to avoid and respond to a relapse of disordered behavior.

Drug Treatments

In some cases, prescription drugs are used to treat eating disorders—usually in combination with some other form of therapy. Many individuals affected by eating disorders are

Because many people with eating disorders also suffer from mental disorders such as depression, anxiety, and bipolar disorder, doctors often prescribe medication as part of treatment.

also diagnosed with other psychological disorders, such as depression, bipolar disorder, and anxiety disorders. Some doctors prescribe medication to treat those ailments in the hope that it may also improve a patient's disordered eating behavior. For anorexia, a range of different drugs can figure into treatment, including those commonly used to reduce depression, psychotic behavior, and anxiety, as well as medications designed to improve appetite and digestion. Antidepressants are also used to treat bulimia and binge-eating disorder. In addition, patients with binge-eating disorder are sometimes prescribed drugs that are used in the treatment of obesity and epilepsy.

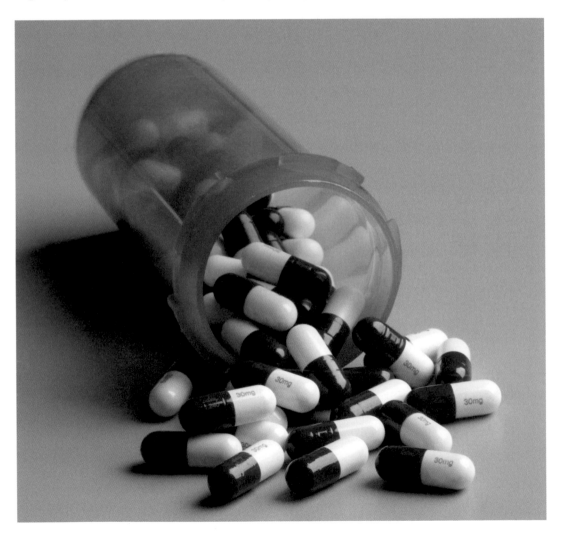

The effectiveness of drug treatment varies, depending on the disorder in question. Research indicates that medications do not significantly help anorexic patients to gain weight or improve their disordered behavior, but antidepressants have been proven to help some recovering patients avoid a relapse. With regard to bulimia, most studies have found that antidepressants are somewhat effective in helping patients to avoid bingeing and purging and avoiding relapses. Fewer studies have been conducted on drug treatments for binge-eating disorder. The results attained thus far indicate that medications can be an effective option, although some of the drugs have significant side effects.

The High Cost of Care

Whatever type of treatment a person receives for an eating disorder, the cost can be extremely high. The average cost of residential treatment is thirty thousand dollars per month, for instance, and many patients must spend several months in that type of facility. The expense prevents most people from being able to afford professional care for an eating disorder without some type of medical insurance coverage. Historically, though, insurance plans in the United States have provided far less coverage for the treatment of mental disorders than for physical ailments. This issue was addressed to a certain degree by mental health parity legislation passed by Congress in 2008, but certain restrictions put in place by insurance providers can still create difficulties for those seeking help for a family member with an eating disorder.

Individuals who seek treatment for an eating disorder need to check the details of the coverage provided by their health insurance plan. They may also want to consult with

HEALTH FACT

Many eating-disorder specialists believe that it is helpful for a recovering patient to resume normal activities, such as work or school studies, as soon as possible after treatment. Individuals who have received treatment in hospitals or residential care facilities are often encouraged to return to their usual activities immediately after being released.

organizations dedicated to assisting people affected by eating disorders. Such groups may be able to offer advice on the best course of action to follow in order to obtain coverage. These organizations are also a good resource for those who have no health insurance, as they provide useful information about treatment resources available to the uninsured.

Treatment programs, which typically extend over a period of at least several months, can help people with eating

Costs for residential treatment of eating disorders average thirty thousand dollars a month.

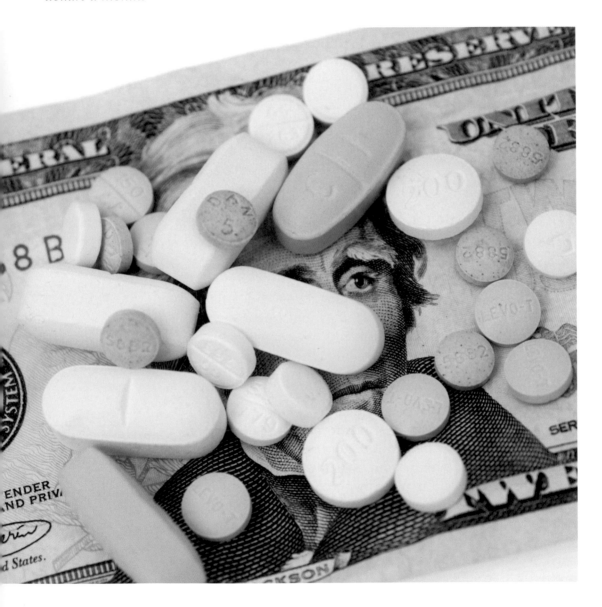

disorders address the underlying causes of their illness, to learn valuable coping skills, and to achieve a more stable way of life. Completion of a single treatment program, however, does not mean that the individual has been "cured" of his or her eating disorder. Many patients who complete a specific program must then continue their treatment through ongoing psychological counseling or by attending meetings of an eating-disorder support group. Full recovery is a long-term project, and most patients will find that their progress is accompanied by setbacks. Relapses are very common, and patients and their families need to keep a realistic perspective about the difficulties they will encounter.

CHAPTER 5

Living with an Eating Disorder

People who complete a treatment program for an eating disorder often find themselves in a much improved condition. At that point, the patient and his or her family and friends may believe that the danger has passed and life will to return to normal. In reality, though, recovery is a never-ending journey. As Tara M. Rio explains in *The Anorexia Diaries,* permanently overcoming an eating disorder requires a great deal of time and effort:

> I walked out of the hospital physically and emotionally drained from the intensive treatment, but I was certain the worst was over. . . . Reintegrating myself into my former life was much harder than I anticipated. It was like learning to walk and talk all over again. . . . I had to retrain my mind to handle life's daily problems in a completely different way, a much harder way. I now had to cope with problems instead of stuffing them down or throwing them up, and I had no idea how hard that was going to be.[23]

The Long Road of Recovery

To truly recover from an eating disorder, patients need to make profound changes in how they feel about themselves, how they relate to food, and how they deal with stress and other factors that may have contributed to their disorders. In essence, they need to gain new insights into their personality and to fundamentally alter their way of life. Such large-scale change is very frightening, and it involves much more than following a diet plan for a few months and attending psychotherapy sessions.

Continuing therapy sessions after completing an eating-disorder treatment program can be very helpful in managing stress.

Many people affected by eating disorders took up their disordered behavior in the first place as a response to some profound source of stress in their life. It can be extremely difficult to give up that coping mechanism, as harmful as it

may have been. Continuing with psychological counseling and therapy sessions after completing a treatment program can be very helpful in this regard. These resources can assist patients in finding new methods to manage stress without returning to their previous self-destructive food-related behavior.

Another factor affecting recovery is that an eating disorder can become a deeply ingrained part of a person's identity, particularly for those who are affected for many years before seeking treatment. As a result, many patients find the recovery process—which requires them to give up a part of who they are—to be a frightening process. "You've just got this stereotype of yourself," one patient explains, "and you think that if you're not the girl with anorexia, then who are you? You don't know how to be anything else."[24]

The Danger of Relapse

Given the significant challenges faced by people in recovery from an eating disorder, it is not surprising that patients frequently experience a relapse. Essentially, relapse means that a patient returns to the harmful actions that were part of his or her eating disorder. Defining precisely what constitutes a relapse can be difficult, because such behavior can vary in intensity and duration. Generally, the term is used when individuals resume their disordered behavior for an extended period of time—several weeks or longer.

In many cases, a relapse results from some type of stressful situation. The patient responds to stress by retreating to the eating disorder that he or she previously used to cope with difficulties. "I know there are certain triggers that set me off," notes one woman who has struggled with bulimia. "One is being in a very social situation, like a party or a club. I feel uncomfortable, especially in cases where people are giving each other the once-over. . . . Because I know I'm not measuring up. I'm very aware of my body, very nervous. And so I find that when these situations occur, I purge."[25] Sudden variations in the routines a patient has established during recovery can also bring about a relapse. For example, a patient in recovery who travels away from home may find that the resulting changes in schedule and meal preparation, along with the stress that comes with unfamiliar surroundings, can prompt disordered behavior to recur.

Sometimes relapses can occur when eating-disorder patients begin making small changes in their diet plan, such as substituting an apple for a full breakfast.

In other cases, the relapse may be more of a gradual process that does not stem from an easily identifiable triggering event. The patient may begin making small changes in his or her diet plan, eating just an apple for breakfast, for instance, rather than a full meal of cereal, fruit, and juice. These actions may progress to skipping occasional meals. Before long, the affected individual becomes caught up in old patterns of disordered eating and other related behavior. Another common experience is that patients make good progress in recovery, but they come to believe that they have put on a bit too much weight in the process. When they attempt to trim just a few pounds, the situation quickly spirals out of control and their eating disorder reasserts itself with a vengeance.

One of the keys to successfully managing a relapse is to understand that it is very common among people battling eating disorders. In fact, a relapse can be considered a difficult step along the road to recovery. Rather than becoming greatly upset about what happened and losing all hope of getting better, a patient suffering a relapse should seek help from his or her therapist as soon as possible and then return to the treatment plan that has been established. Although the experience can be disheartening, a relapse also offers an opportunity for learning, as it can help the patient to identify and avoid the factors that contributed to the return of disordered behavior. "I told myself that this was probably normal . . . and that I shouldn't beat myself up about it," a patient recovering from bulimia says of the relapse she experienced.

> I was getting so mad at myself for doing it that that was creating more anxiety about the whole thing. So I just had to say, "I'm not bulimic again. I'm just having problems dealing with some things." . . . And I made some phone calls to therapists. And just the idea of getting myself out of it, just starting to climb out of the hole made me keep going.[26]

Because recovery is so difficult and the potential for relapse is so high, some experts suggest that patients should not expect to reach a point when their eating disorder is completely a thing of the past. Instead, these authorities

Treatment Versus Cure

Research suggests that eating disorders can be effectively treated, but although individuals may overcome eating disorders and go on to lead healthy lives, they must always remain vigilant to avoid a relapse. "Treatment can help an individual lessen her symptoms (restricting, purging, and so on) and obtain a better quality of life. However, treatment does not cure an eating disorder," Nicole Johns explains in *Purge: Rehab Diaries*. "What the general public does not realize is that the eating-disordered individual struggles and needs continued support after leaving treatment, and that, to some extent, she will struggle with eating disorder urges after treatment, even if she doesn't act on them. The happily-ever-after ending of many of the eating disorder books on the market today is a myth."

Nicole Johns. *Purge: Rehab Diaries*. Berkeley, CA: Seal, 2009, p. 8.

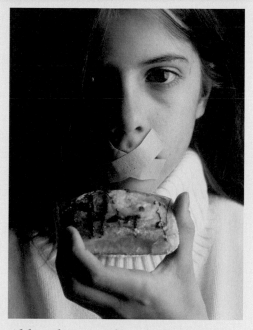

Although eating disorders can be effectively treated and patients can go on to lead normal lives, they must remain vigilant to avoid relapses.

argue that eating disorders should be viewed in the same way as diabetes and alcoholism: as diseases that can be effectively treated and controlled, but that cannot be completely cured.

Recovery Statistics

Statistics about the number of individuals who successfully recover from eating disorders can vary greatly from source to source. The following figures offer a general overview based on the findings of a number of studies. Most analyses of recovery look at the different types of eating disorders separately. This approach shows that a patient's odds of success vary greatly depending on the type of disorder he or she has.

Anorexia nervosa is the most difficult eating disorder to overcome. Studies have shown that about half of anorexia patients achieve full recovery. Another one-third of patients are able to improve their condition, though they still experience some aspects of the disorder, including low body weight and persistent psychological issues related to body image. In addition, incidents of relapse are extremely common with anorexia. Research has indicated that even among patients who appear to have achieved a full recovery, one of every three later suffers a relapse. Not all anorexia cases are the same, of course, and certain factors can significantly affect a person's chances of recovery. For instance, research has shown that patients who have been affected by the disorder for a relatively short time before beginning treatment are better able to overcome anorexia. This statistic underscores the importance of seeking help as soon as possible. In addition, younger patients and those who have experienced only limited weight loss tend to respond better to treatment.

Individuals with bulimia nervosa are more likely to overcome their eating disorder. One study that looked at bulimia patients over the course of ninety months showed that nearly three-quarters had experienced a full recovery. Another research project put the figure closer to 70 percent. On a less positive note, studies have also shown that some patients can struggle with aspects of bulimia for many years. Such individuals often experience up-and-down cycles, with times of marked improvement interspersed with multiple serious relapses.

There has been relatively little research into the recovery statistics for those diagnosed with eating disorder not otherwise specified (EDNOS). One of the few studies available found that nearly 60 percent of patients recovered from their disorder over the course of two years. Research results into binge-eating disorder (BED) have varied, though one study that examined relatively young BED patients found that their rate of recovery was better than that of bulimia patients. That same analysis noted that even though many individuals were able to overcome their binge eating, they were less successful when it came to losing weight. As a result, they continued to experience obesity.

While these statistics provide some useful insight into the likelihood of recovery over the short term, they do not offer much information about a patient's potential for long-term success. Only a few research projects have tracked eating-disorder patients for a decade or more. One well-known ongoing study has been conducted by doctors at Massachusetts General Hospital since the late 1980s. It monitors 246 people, around half of whom were affected by anorexia and half by bulimia. So far, the results indicate that about one-third of the patients have made a full

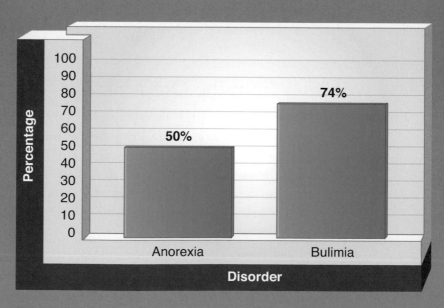

Percentages of Anorexia and Bulimia Patients Attaining Full Recovery

Taken from: Carlos M. Grilo, *Eating and Weight Disorders*, Hove, UK: Psychology, 2006, pp. 42–43.

One study showed that over the course of ninety months nearly three-quarters of bulimia patients experienced a full recovery.

recovery; another one-third have shown improvement but have experienced up-and-down cycles; and the final third have made little progress.

Views from the Other Side: Reflections on Recovery

Individuals who have successfully recovered from eating disorders often recount their experiences in similar ways. Such accounts make it clear that despite daunting challenges, the recovery process offers lifelong benefits. People who overcome eating disorders can still build full, rewarding, and healthy lives for themselves.

Many people who succeed in recovery recall reaching a stage wherein they recognized that they simply could no longer continue with the unhealthy way of life they had known. This change in attitude carries immense importance, but it does not necessarily arrive in a single, dramatic instant, as it might in a movie or television program. "There was no revelatory moment," notes Marya Hornbacher in her memoir *Wasted*. "Mostly what happened was that my life took over—that is to say, that the impulse for life became stronger in me than the impulse for death."[27]

A similar epiphany occurred for Lisa Himmel, who recounts her experiences in the book *Hungry*. After years of struggling to overcome her bulimia and anorexia with different types of treatment, she finally became convinced that she could beat her disease. "What has really changed is that I believe that I can continue to improve and reach as much of a full recovery as possible. I no longer have the *desire* to starve or diet and binge and purge. . . . I'm not willing to make myself suffer anymore. There is no discharge from my treatment plan. All I know is that I see a new strength in me—a strength I had forgotten."[28]

Finding New Roads

Patients with eating disorders typically find that it takes great determination and repeated attempts to break the cycle of disordered behavior and establish healthy eating habits. "My disorder was a path I'd created early on and worn through use into a superhighway. It seemed like the only way I had to go," recalls Cindy Bitter. "But it only led [to] one place, and that was death. Recovery was all about clearing new paths to healthier destinations, using them and reusing them until these new roads were as wide open as the old, disordered one. If I stayed off that old highway long enough, it would get so overgrown it wasn't accessible anymore. That's why recovery was so hard at first, but also why it got easier and easier as I kept at it."

Quoted in Amy Liu. *Gaining: The Truth About Life After Eating Disorders.* New York: Warner, 2007, p. 256.

Many of those who make an extended recovery experience one or more serious relapses along the way. Rather than give up in the face of these setbacks, however, people who successfully manage their eating disorders remain focused on their goal and rely on the skills and knowledge they have gained in treatment. Marianne Apostolides admits that "I will probably relapse again," but adds that "when I do, I will

People can successfully manage their eating disorders and remain focused on their goals with the skills and knowledge they have gained in treatment.

know how to deal with it: with the recognition that relapses are part of the process of letting go, with compassion for myself as I go through this difficult part of the process, and with the knowledge that I can bring myself back to a place of emotional and physical health."[29]

There is no surefire way to find that kind of resolve, but other people who have recovered from eating disorders can often be a source of strength and inspiration. Their accounts of conviction and perseverance can be a powerful source of hope to all those who struggle with an eating disorder. Above all else, the essential element in making a successful recovery is determination—the strength to continue striving toward a better way of life, regardless of the obstacles. As one woman relates in *Sensing the Self: Women's Recovery from Bulimia:*

> It was so miserable for me that last year that I could not persist with the status quo. I remember sitting in the therapist's office. . . . I felt really by myself. And as terrifying . . . as that was, I remember thinking, . . . "If I don't drive, no one else will." Like no one's gonna do this for me. . . . And as hard as it was going to be, I was going to have to drive. I remember building that courage. 'Cause I would get scared, but I remember just that I had to. I had to do it.[30]

NOTES

Chapter 1: Eating Disorders and the People They Affect

1. Nicole Johns. *Purge: Rehab Diaries.* Berkeley, CA: Seal, 2009, p. 20.
2. Pamela Carlton and Deborah Ashin. *Take Charge of Your Child's Eating Disorder: A Physician's Step-by-Step Guide to Defeating Anorexia and Bulimia.* New York: Marlowe, 2007, p. 4.
3. Hilde Bruch. *The Golden Cage: The Enigma of Anorexia Nervosa.* Cambridge, MA: Harvard University Press, 2001, p. xxi.
4. Quoted in Bruch. *The Golden Cage,* p. xix.
5. Carlos M. Grilo. *Eating and Weight Disorders.* Hove, UK: Psychology, 2006, pp. 36–37.
6. Bruch. *The Golden Cage,* p. xx.

Chapter 2: Types, Characteristics, and Dangers of Eating Disorders

7. Trisha Gura. *Lying in Weight: The Hidden Epidemic of Eating Disorders in Adult Women.* New York: HarperCollins, 2007, p. xii.
8. Carrie Arnold, with Timothy B. Walsh, MD. *Next to Nothing: A Firsthand Account of One Teenager's Experience with an Eating Disorder.* New York: Oxford University Press, 2007, p. 29.
9. Quoted in Suzanne Abraham. *Eating Disorders: The Facts.* 6th ed. Oxford, UK: Oxford University Press, 2008, p. 27.
10. *Diagnostic and Statistical Manual of Mental Disorders.* 4th ed. Washington, DC: American Psychological Association, 2000, p. 594.
11. *Diagnostic and Statistical Manual of Mental Disorders,* p. 594.
12. Alexander R. Lucas. *Demystifying Anorexia Nervosa: An Optimistic Guide to Understanding and Healing.* New York: Oxford University Press, 2004, pp. 9–10.
13. Ilana Kurshan. "To Poison an Ideal." In *Going Hungry: Writers on Desire, Self-Denial, and Overcoming Anorexia,* edited by Kate Taylor. New York: Anchor, 2008, p. 35.

Chapter 3: Causes and Risk Factors

14. Quoted in Christine Halse, Anne Honey, and Desiree Boughtwood.

Inside Anorexia: The Experiences of Girls and Their Families. London: Jessica Kingsley, 2008, p. 36.

15. Jennifer Egan. "Daughters of the Diet Revolution." In *Going Hungry: Writers on Desire, Self-Denial, and Overcoming Anorexia*, edited by Kate Taylor. New York: Anchor, 2008, p. 51.

16. John Nolan. "Hungry Men." In *Going Hungry: Writers on Desire, Self-denial, and Overcoming Anorexia*, edited by Kate Taylor. New York: Anchor, 2008, p. 75.

17. Quoted in Halse, Honey, and Boughtwood. *Inside Anorexia*, p. 45.

18. Quoted in Sheila M. Reindl. *Sensing the Self: Women's Recovery from Bulimia*. Cambridge, MA: Harvard University Press, 2011, p. 14.

19. Sheila Himmel and Lisa Himmel. *Hungry: A Mother and Daughter Fight Anorexia*. New York: Berkley, 2009, p. 169.

Chapter 4: Treatment of Eating Disorders

20. Marianne Apostolides. *Inner Hunger: A Young Woman's Struggle Through Anorexia and Bulimia*. New York: Norton, 1998, p. 158.

21. Quoted in June Alexander, with Professor Daniel Le Grange. *My Kid Is Back: Empowering Parents to Beat Anorexia Nervosa*. London: Routledge, 2010, pp. 38–39.

22. Grilo. *Eating and Weight Disorders*, p. 109.

Chapter 5: Living with an Eating Disorder

23. Linda M. Rio and Tara M. Rio, with Craig Johnson, PhD. *The Anorexia Diaries: A Mother and Daughter's Triumph Over Teenage Eating Disorders*. Emmaus, PA: Rodale, 2003, p. 129.

24. Quoted in Halse, Honey, and Boughtwood. *Inside Anorexia*, p. 77.

25. Quoted in Gail B. Stewart. *Teens with Eating Disorders*. San Diego: Lucent, 2001, pp. 30–31.

26. Quoted in Reindl. *Sensing the Self*, p. 255.

27. Marya Hornbacher. *Wasted: A Memoir of Anorexia and Bulimia*. New York: HarperPerennial, 1999, p. 280.

28. Himmel and Himmel. *Hungry*, p. 274.

29. Apostolides. *Inner Hunger*, pp. 137–38.

30. Quoted in Reindl. *Sensing the Self*, p. 73.

amenorrhea: The absence of a menstrual period in females who have attained sexual maturity; it is one of the symptoms used to make a clinical diagnosis of anorexia nervosa in sexually mature women.

anorexia nervosa: An eating disorder in which affected individuals severely restrict their diet until they become extremely underweight. People with anorexia have a severe fear of gaining weight and a disturbed perception of their weight and body shape so that they are unable to accurately assess their physical condition. Anorexia is sometimes made worse by excessive exercise and by purging (vomiting or misusing laxatives, diuretics, and enemas).

binge-eating disorder (BED): An eating disorder in which affected individuals engage in uncontrolled eating binges but do not attempt to eliminate the calories consumed through purging, excessive exercise, or fasting, as is the case with bulimia nervosa.

bulimia nervosa: An eating disorder in which affected individuals engage in uncontrolled eating binges and then attempt to eliminate the calories consumed through purging, excessive exercise, or fasting. People with bulimia are obsessed with their weight and the appearance of their bodies and allow these factors to have a very large effect on the way they feel about themselves.

cognitive behavioral therapy (CBT): A type of psychotherapy treatment that focuses on correcting the destructive cycle of behavior demonstrated by those with eating disorders.

DSM: The abbreviation for the *Diagnostic and Statistical Manual of Mental Disorders*, a book published by the American Psychological Association that lists all of the officially recognized psychological disorders and defines them with specific criteria.

eating disorder not otherwise specified (EDNOS): A category of eating disorders that covers behavior that does not fit the full medical definition for a diagnosis of anorexia nervosa or bulimia nervosa.

female athlete triad: A medical condition sometimes found among elite female athletes who attempt to lose weight in order to improve their performance in a particular sport; symptoms include disordered eating, amenorrhea or loss of period, and osteoporosis or bone loss.

Maudsley method: A type of psychotherapy treatment that has proven effective for individuals with eating disorders; family members are actively involved in assisting the patient to improve his or her condition and to overcome disordered behavior.

osteoporosis: A loss of bone density; the condition is often found in elderly women, but it can also affect people with eating disorders who experience severe malnutrition.

prevalence: The proportion of the general population that is affected by a certain medical condition.

purging: Eliminating food from the body by self-induced vomiting or by misusing laxatives, diuretics, and enemas.

relapse: A return to disordered behavior following a period of improvement.

Academy for Eating Disorders (AED)

111 Deer Lake Rd., Ste. 100
Deerfield, IL 60015
Phone: (847) 498-4274
Website: www.aedweb.org/

The AED is an organization for professionals involved in eating disorder treatment and research. Its website includes information and resources for the general public.

Beat: Beating Eating Disorders

Wensum House
103 Prince of Wales Rd.
Norwich, Norfolk NR1 1DW
Phone: 0845 634 1414 (adult helpline); 0845 634 7650 (youth helpline)
Website: www.b-eat.co.uk/

This British-based charity provides information, assistance, and online message boards to help adults and youth with eating disorders.

Eating Disorders Anonymous (EDA)

PO Box 55876
Phoenix, AZ 85078-5876
Website: www.eatingdisordersanonymous.org/

EDA is a fellowship of individuals who seek to support one another in the recovery process. It operates in a manner similar to Alcoholics Anonymous, and its website offers information and a listing of local EDA meetings.

Harris Center for Education and Advocacy in Eating Disorders

2 Longfellow Pl., Ste. 200
Boston, MA. 02114
Phone: (617) 726-8470
Website: www.harriscentermgh.org/

The Harris Center is a well-known treatment center at Massachusetts General Hospital. Its website includes tips on how parents and teachers can assist young people with eating disorders as well as other useful information.

Maudsley Parents

Website: www.maudsleyparents.org/

This volunteer organization offers detailed information on family-based treatment for eating disorders, such as the Maudsley method, as well as a directory of treatment providers.

National Association of Anorexia Nervosa and Associated Disorders (ANAD)

PO Box 640
Naperville, IL 60566
Phone: (630) 577-1330
Website: www.anad.org/

ANAD offers assistance to individuals affected by anorexia nervosa, bulimia nervosa, and binge-eating disorder via telephone, e-mail, and an online forum. It also puts individuals in touch with support groups and treatment providers.

National Eating Disorder Information Centre-Canada (NEDIC)

ES 7-421, 200 Elizabeth St.
Toronto, Ontario M5G 2C4
Phone: (866) 633-4220
Website: www.nedic.ca/

This Canadian nonprofit organization provides information and resources on eating disorders and food and weight preoccupation. Its services include a toll-free telephone helpline.

National Eating Disorders Association (NEDA)

165 West 46th St.
New York, NY 10036
Phone: (800) 931-2237
Website: www.nationaleatingdisorders.org/

NEDA provides information and assistance to individuals and families affected by eating disorders. It also serves as an advocate for prevention, improved treatment, and increased research funding.

Overeaters Anonymous (OA)

PO Box 44020
Rio Rancho, NM 87174-4020
Phone: (505) 891-2664
Website: www.oa.org/

This fellowship organization focuses on recovery from compulsive overeating, but it also deals with other aspects of disordered behavior related to food. Its website provides contact information for local OA meetings.

Books

June Alexander, with Daniel Le Grange. *My Kid Is Back: Empowering Parents to Beat Anorexia Nervosa.* London: Routledge, 2010. This book details the experiences of ten youths with anorexia nervosa who were treated with the Maudsley method.

Toney Allman. *Eating Disorders.* Farmington Hills, MI: Lucent, 2010. This book offers an overview of the subject in a format accessible to young readers.

Carrie Arnold, with Timothy B. Walsh, MD. *Next to Nothing: A Firsthand Account of One Teenager's Experience with an Eating Disorder.* New York: Oxford University Press, 2007. This thorough guide to treatment is based on Arnold's own struggle with eating disorders.

Joyce Brennfleck, ed. *Eating Disorders Sourcebook.* 2nd edition. Detroit: Omnigraphics, 2007. This book provides a comprehensive anthology of information on eating disorders.

Hilde Bruch. *The Golden Cage: The Enigma of Anorexia Nervosa*, Cambridge, MA: Harvard University Press, 2001. *The Golden Cage* is an early and important study of anorexia by one of the pioneers of eating-disorder research.

Pamela Carlton and Deborah Ashin. *Take Charge of Your Child's Eating Disorder: A Physician's Step-by-Step Guide to Defeating Anorexia and Bulimia.* New York: Marlowe, 2007. Designed primarily for use by parents, this book offers an overview of eating disorders and treatment options.

Christina Chiu. *Eating Disorder Survivors Tell Their Stories.* New York: Rosen, 1998. Chiu's book profiles four young people who are affected by different types of eating disorders, including anorexia and bulimia.

Christine Halse, Anne Honey, and Desiree Boughtwood. *Inside Anorexia: The Experiences of Girls and Their Families.* London: Jessica Kingsley, 2008. This book offers an overview of anorexia as well as numerous accounts of patients and their families.

Nicole Johns. *Purge: Rehab Diaries.* Berkeley, CA: Seal, 2009. *Purge* is a compelling memoir of a young woman's experiences with an eating disorder not otherwise specified (EDNOS) and her treatment at a residential facility.

Paul R. Robbins, PhD. *Anorexia and Bulimia.* Springfield, NJ: Enslow, 1998. Robbins provides a thorough look at eating disorders in an easy-to-read style designed for young readers.

Judy Tam Sargent. *The Long Road Back: A Survivor's Guide to Anorexia.* Georgetown, MA: North Star, 1999. Sargent's memoir describes her struggle with anorexia and her journey toward recovery.

Gail B. Stewart. *Teens with Eating Disorders.* San Diego: Lucent, 2001. This book provides biographies of four individuals affected by eating disorders of various types.

Website

National Institute of Mental Health, "Eating Disorders." (www.nimh.nih.gov/health/publications/eating-disorders/complete-index.shtml). This online resource provides a brief overview of the types of eating disorders, their symptoms and side effects, and treatment options.

INDEX

A

Amenorrhea, 31, 40

American Psychological Association, 28

Anorexia nervosa
  age of onset, 19
  diagnostic criteria for, 29–33
  first identification of, 8, 15–16
  percentage of patients recovery from, *83*
  physical effects of, *40*
  prevalence of, 23
  recovery statistics on, 82
  woman with, *25*

Anxiety disorders, 51

Apostolides, Marianne, 60, 86

B

Binge-eating disorder (BED), 14–15, 32
  age of onset, 19
  bulimia *vs.,* 36
  cognitive-behavioral therapy and, 69–71
  recovery statistics on, 82–83

Blood problems, 39

Body image, inaccurate, 29–30, *31,* 49, 82

Bone problems, 41, *41*

Brain
  impacts of malnutrition on, 39, 42
  role in eating disorders, 56, 59

Bruch, Hilde, 13

Bulimia nervosa
  binge-eating disorder *vs.,* 36
  cognitive-behavioral therapy and, 69–71
  diagnostic criteria for, 33–35
  first recognition of, 16
  percentage of patients recovering from, *83*
  prevalence of, 24–25
  recovery statistics on, 82
  types of, 35

C

Carpenter, Karen, 17

Catherine of Siena (saint), 15

CBT (cognitive-behavioral therapy), 69–71

Centers for Disease Control and Prevention (CDC), 30
  on percentage of people who want to lose weight, 13

Cognitive problems, 39

Cognitive-behavioral therapy (CBT), 69–71

PICTURE CREDITS

Jeff Hill is a freelance writer based in Austin, Texas. He is the author of *Defining Moments: Prohibition, Defining Moments: Women's Suffrage*, and *The Holocaust* and is the coauthor of *Life Events and Rites of Passage*. He has contributed to a variety of historical and literary reference works, including *The Persian Gulf War, The Industrial Revolution in America*, and *Biography Today*. In addition, his travel-related writing has been published by Lonely Planet, *Travel Weekly*, and *Weissmann Travel Reports*.